Amsterdam
Shortlist

timeout.com / amsterdam

151

115

Contents

98

ABOUT THE GUIDE

The *Time Out Amsterdam Shortlist* is one of a series of pocket guides to cities around the globe. Drawing on the expertise of local authors, it distils their knowledge into a handy, easy-to-use format that ensures you get the most from your trip, whether you're a first-time or a return visitor.

Time Out Amsterdam Shortlist is divided into four sections:

Welcome to Amsterdam introduces the city and provides inspiration for your visit.

Amsterdam Day by Day helps you plan your trip with an events calendar and customised itineraries.

Amsterdam by Area is the main visitor section of the guide. It includes detailed listings and reviews for the very best sights, museums, restaurants ⑩, bars ⑩, shops ⑩ and entertainment venues ⑩, all organised by area with a corresponding street map. To help navigation, each area of Barcelona has been assigned its own colour.

Amsterdam Essentials provides practical visitor information, including accommodation options and details of public transport.

Shortlists & highlights

We have selected a Shortlist of stand-out venues in each area, which are marked with a heart ♥ in the text. The very best of these appear in the Highlights feature (*see p10*) and receive extended coverage in the guide.

Maps

There's an overview map on *p8* and individual street maps for each area of the city. Venues featured in the guide have been given a grid reference so that you can find them easily on the maps and on the ground.

Prices

All our **restaurant** listings are marked with a euro symbol (€-€€€€) indicating the average price you should expect to pay for a main course in Amsterdam: € = under €10; €€ = €10-€20; €€€ = €20-€30; €€€€ = over €30.

A similar system is used in our **Accommodation** chapter, based on the hotel's standard prices for one night in a double room: Budget = under €100; Mid-range = €100-€200; Expensive = €200-€300; Luxury = over €300.

Introduction

Cobblestone streets, gabled houses and impossibly quaint canals: Amsterdam's physical appeal is undeniable. But the Dutch city's allure runs deeper than its attractive surface (which, by the way, is held up by over 10 million wooden poles sunk deep into the mud). While Amsterdam's photogenic looks will always be a draw, it's what the snaps don't capture that makes it truly unique. Liberalism and open-mindedness reign supreme in this city, resulting in an international reputation for anything-goes hedonism. The coffeeshops and sex shops are inducement enough for some, but it's the creative energy of the city's inhabitants that should really inspire you to visit.

Whether you're into culture, food, design or partying until the wee hours, Amsterdam delivers the buzz of a big city in a small space. Its internationally acclaimed museums, including the Van Gogh Museum and Rijksmuseum, are just a short cycle away from the Red Light District, 24-hour nightclubs, inventive restaurants and peaceful parks. Whether you're on a flying visit or a more leisurely holiday, you'll find there's more to Amsterdam than coffeeshops and canals.

Welcome to Amsterdam

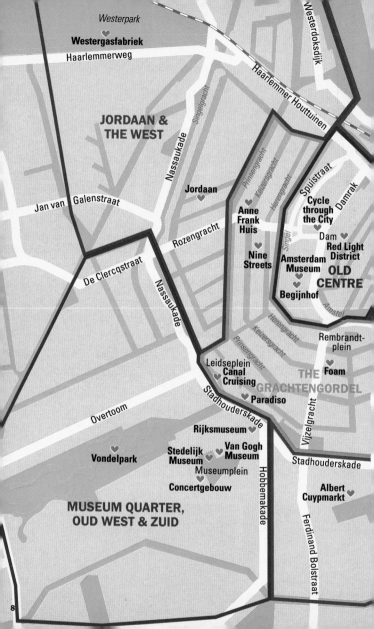

Westerpark

Westergasfabriek

Haarlemmerweg

Haarlemmer Houttuinen

Westerdoksdijk

**JORDAAN &
THE WEST**

Nassaukade

Singelgracht

Jan van Galenstraat

Jordaan ♥

Prinsengracht

Keizersgracht

Herengracht

Spuistraat

Damrak

**Cycle
through
the City** ♥

Rozengracht

**Anne
Frank
Huis** ♥

Singel

Dam ♥

**Red Light
District**

**OLD
CENTRE**

De Clercqstraat

**Nine
Streets** ♥

**Amsterdam
Museum** ♥

Nassaukade

Begijnhof ♥

Amstel

Herengracht

Keizersgracht

Rembrandt-
plein

Prinsengracht

Leidseplein ♥
**Canal
Cruising**

**THE
GRACHTENGORDEL**

♥ **Foam**

Vijzelgracht

♥ **Paradiso**

Overtoom

Stadhouderskade

Rijksmuseum ♥

Hobbemakade

**Stedelijk
Museum** ♥

♥ **Van Gogh
Museum**

Stadhouderskade

Vondelpark ♥

Museumplein

Concertgebouw ♥

**Albert
Cuypmarkt** ♥

**MUSEUM QUARTER,
OUD WEST & ZUID**

Ferdinand Bolstraat

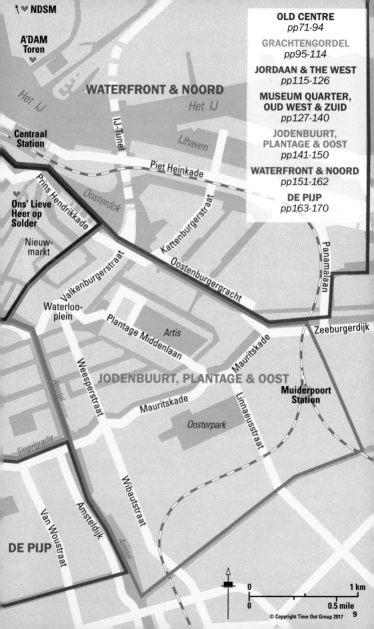

© Copyright Time Out Group 2017

Highlights

Amsterdam manages to maintain its laid-back local vibe, while at the same time attracting increasing numbers of international visitors. From Anne Frank to Van Gogh, and the Rijksmuseum to the Red Light District, we count down the highlights of this historical merchant city turned thriving 21st-century metropolis.

01

Canal cruising *p98*

Amsterdam's UNESCO-protected canals are as rich in history as they are charming. Picturesque passages of water entwining quaint cobblestoned streets paint the global image of this unique city, and the eel's eye view is the best way to see it for yourself. Guided tours run through the historical Grachtengordel canal belt. If you're feeling energetic, hire a canal bike for up to four people from outside Anne Frank Huis.

Van Gogh Museum *p137*

The world may be awash with Van Gogh copies but there's nothing quite like admiring the real thing – just ask the 1.6 million-plus people who visit this museum every year. The permanent exhibition features some 200 paintings and 500 drawings by Van Gogh, and temporary shows explore his contemporaries and his influence on other artists. Avoid the queues by booking tickets online, or visit around noon or late afternoon.

03

Anne Frank Huis *p100*

One of the 20th century's most famous authors was dead at 15. Her book, *The Diary of Anne Frank*, documented the two years her Jewish family spent hiding from the Nazis in a small backhouse. After being betrayed, the family members were sent to concentration camps, and only her father survived. The family's preserved hiding place and the accompanying exhibitions resonate with a simple message – 'Never again' – which is as relevant as ever.

04

Red Light District *p76*

Yes, it's a red-light district where women get paid for sex. But Amsterdam's sleaze zone also remains one of the city's oldest neighbourhoods, and contains many ancient houses, squares and churches, along with nurseries, schools and locals going about their business. Chief annoyance: roving packs of drunken British stag partygoers – oh, the shame.

05

Cycle through the city *p70*

They don't call it the city on two wheels for nothing. There are more than 800,000 bicycles in Amsterdam, almost more than the city's population. Cycling is a quintessential part of Amsterdam culture and by far the cheapest and easiest way to get around. Pedal through the city's photogenic Grachtengordel and scenic paths of Vondelpark. A guided cycle tour is a great way to see the city.

06

Vondelpark *p138*

In the 1970s KLM airways lured American longhairs to visit Amsterdam with the slogan: 'Come sleep in Hippie Park'. Today, Vondelpark is merely a people's park and the city's green lung. On sunny days and Sundays, it becomes the most densely populated spot in the city. During the summer, you'll likely hear the echo of bass from whatever pop-up festival is being held in the park.

07

A'DAM Toren *p153*

Standing proudly in Amsterdam's Noord is the A'DAM Toren, previously home to oil company Royal Dutch Shell until 2009. After a multi-million-euro facelift, the landmark reopened in 2016 as a multifunctional hub, complete with offices, cafés, restaurants, music rooms, a nightclub and rooftop terrace. For an unrivalled view of the city, the A'DAM Lookout boasts a 360° panorama and the highest swing in Europe.

08

Rijksmuseum *p130*

The Rijksmuseum's palatial interior – all gold leaf and intricate art nouveau woodwork and patterns – is worthy of a day's admiration in itself. As for the artworks, you'll need a week and it's reassuring to discover that Rembrandt's *The Night Watch* and Vermeer's *The Milkmaid* are not at all overrated. If you're lucky, you'll be greeted by a busker bellowing opera in the vaulted bike path running through the building.

09

Albert Cuypmarkt *p168*

Amsterdam's most famous street market, the 'Cuyp' is a must for anyone looking to bag a bargain or simply soak up the lively Dutch atmosphere. From Monday to Saturday, the wide street is lined with stalls selling everything from crazy wigs to local delicacies, including raw herring and *stroopwafels*. Treat yourself to a stroll around lively De Pijp afterwards.

10

Stroll through the Jordaan *p118*

The laid-back Jordaan is a perfect place for a spot of aimless wandering. Higgledy-piggledy streets offer a surprise round almost every corner: it may be a seemingly forgotten café, a hip art gallery or a window into a living room filled with plain weird stuff. In fact, a semi-random approach can also be applied to the rest of Amsterdam, with its eternally looping streets. Just keep an eye out for the bikes.

11

Stedelijk Museum *p134*

With approximately 90,000 works of art and objects dating back to 1870, the Stedelijk is the largest museum of modern and contemporary art in the country, showcasing movements such as Bauhaus, abstract expressionism and conceptual art to great acclaim. The locals, while visiting in droves, seem to take it a little less seriously – nicknaming the plastic extension the 'bathtub'.

12

Nine Streets *p103*

The UNESCO-crowned Grachtengordel is essential viewing on any visit to Amsterdam, but don't miss the intersecting streets, where most of the city's living, eating and drinking take place. Come with an appetite and a couple of hours. The Nine Streets are where people go to shop – from wonderful cheeses to Karl Lagerfeld's flagship store to 19th-century spectacles to 21st-century denim.

13

Begijnhof *p90*

This hidden courtyard, near the chaos that is high-street shopping strip Kalverstraat, is the perfect place to regain a sense of peace. Just avoid treading on the slab of pink granite by the walkway: it's the grave of a nun and former resident, Cornelia Arents. Begijnhof and its two churches are also handily adjacent to Spui and the freely accessible Civic Guard's Gallery of the Amsterdam Museum.

14

Paradiso *p113*

The Paradiso was once a congregational meeting hall. And, since the 1960s, it's been the 'pop temple' for every relevant genre that followed – from punk to hip hop to dance. The world's biggest musical legends regularly forego a stadium gig to play here. In its smaller upstairs hall, Paradiso books the legends of tomorrow that lure in party-loving locals throughout the week.

15

Westergasfabriek *p123*

The city's vast former gasworks on the western edge of the city were transformed into an award-winning cultural park with clubs, music venues, restaurants, arthouse cinema and plenty of green space, which also plays host to concerts and festivals. Designed by American landscape architect Kathryn Gustafson, Westergasfabriek is a wonderful example of urban reuse.

16

Concertgebouw *p140*

Could this late 19th-century building topped with a shiny golden lyre have the best acoustics on the planet? Sink into one of the comfy seats and decide for yourself as you absorb the sound of world-class orchestras, conductors, ensembles and soloists. If you're already a classical music fan, you undoubtedly have some recordings of the house band, the Royal Concertgebouw Orchestra.

17

Ons' Lieve Heer op Solder *p79*

Translating to 'Museum of Our Lord in the Attic', this 17th-century canal house holds what was once Amsterdam's best kept secret: a church. Built in 1663, the attic church was used by Catholics as a place of worship when they were banned from public prayer after the Alteration. The church has been beautifully preserved and is still used for services and even weddings today.

18

Foam *p110*

The Photography Museum Amsterdam, located in a renovated canal house, displays a comprehensive array of camera-clicking talent. The internationally renowned museum celebrates global photography icons. It also zooms in on the domestic scene by exhibiting work by local photographers, up-and-coming 'Foam Talent', and hosting courses, events and pop-ups. There's an excellent café on site too.

17

19

NDSM *p160*

Once the largest shipyard in Europe, NDSM has redeveloped itself into an 'Art City', with post-industrial architecture and a creative atmosphere on the north bank of the IJ. It is home to restaurants, bars, studios, festivals and cultural venues – including Crane Hotel Faralda (yes, a hotel in an actual crane) and Pllek, an organic restaurant, bar and music venue, complete with manmade urban beach during summer months.

20

Amsterdam Museum *p88*

A couple of hours in this high-tech historical museum will enhance your future wanderings around the city. Marvel at how Amsterdam evolved out of a bog. Respect how local business people gave the middle finger to royalty while creating their own Golden Age. Dig the wacky antics employed by local hippie activists during the 1960s. Raise your eyebrows at how much ecstasy was consumed in the clubbing heyday of the 1990s.

Sightseeing

Technically speaking, Amsterdam shouldn't really exist;
a bog surrounding the River Amstel wasn't ever a natural
support for urban structures. The city is a triumph of
human engineering and a testament to the sheer drive
and ingenuity of its early inhabitants, who built a dam,
created a series of picturesque canal rings to control the
rising waters, and constructed their homes on pilings
driven into the sand. Pluck a cobblestone out of the streets
today and you'll still find seashells right there.

Today, the story of the Dutch capital is told through
its museums and buildings. First and foremost on
any itinerary is the nation's grand treasure house,
the **Rijksmuseum** (*see p130*), which houses the
Netherlands' most important works of art. The

Best viewpoints
Dangle your feet from A'DAM Lookout (*p153*) and gaze across the Old Centre from OBA (*p157*).

Dutch clichés
Have a smoke at Amnesia (*p102*) coffeeshop; buy tulips at Bloemenmarkt (*p111*) and drink beer in the shadow of a windmill at Brouwerij 't IJ (*p148*).

Enter the past
Step back in time at Anne Frank Huis (*p100*), the City Archives (*p107*) and Verzetsmuseum (*p147*).

Back to the future
Stroll around the Waterfront and Noord (*p151*) to see the future of sustainable architecture.

Religious experience
Pay your respects at Nieuwe Kerk (*p89*), Oude Kerk (*p75*) and the Portuguese Synagogue (*p83*).

Most scenic canals
Fill your phone with pictures of Brouwersgracht, Leliegracht and Prinsengracht (*p95*).

Amsterdam Museum (*see p88*) seeks to capture the city's DNA, from the Middle Ages through to the present, while the **Scheepvaartmuseum** (*see p156*) explores 500 years of maritime history. Other temples to the city's rich history and culture include the 800-year-old **Oude Kerk** (*see p75*); **Ons' Lieve Heer op Solder** (*see p79*) – a Catholic church hidden in the attic of a canal house; the **Royal Palace** (*see p87*), and the **Concertgebouw** (*see p140*), with its near-perfect acoustics.

Although Amsterdam was not devastated by bombing, World War II left an indelible mark on the city, especially for the Jewish community. **Anne Frank Huis** (*see p100*), where the famous diarist Anne Frank and her family hid for two years, is now one of Amsterdam's most popular museums. The **Joods Historisch Museum** (*see p146*) provides religious context, while the **Verzetsmuseum** (*see p147*) tells the story of the Dutch Resistance in WWII.

Stedelijk Museum

Artistic tradition

The groundwork for Amsterdam's artistic Golden Age was laid by medieval artists such as Jacob Cornelisz van Oostsanen (c1470-1533), also known as Jacob van Amsterdam, whose sharp observations became a trademark for all Dutch art that was to follow. Look out for his *Saul and the Witch of Endor* on display at the Rijksmuseum.

Once the Golden Age arrived in the 17th century, the aspirant middle classes paid Rembrandt van Rijn, Jan Vermeer, Frans Hals, Ferdinand Bol and Jan Steen (among others) to make art while the money shone. Many of their works are on display in the Rijksmuseum's Gallery of Honour, including Rembrandt's most famous painting, *The Night Watch*, which captures the lively chaos of Amsterdam's Civic Guard. You can also visit the **Rembrandthuis** (*see p146*) to see the artist's old home and etchings.

Fast forward 200 years and it was the turn of everyone's favourite earless genius, Vincent van Gogh (1853-90). Some of his most iconic paintings are exhibited at the **Van Gogh Museum** (*see p137*). And, if that's not enough, the **Stedelijk Museum** (*see p134*), the largest collection of modern and contemporary art in the

Netherlands, is just next door; visit here for work by the likes of Piet Mondrian (1872-1944) and other exponents of the Dutch De Stijl movement.

But art in Amsterdam is not confined to the museums: there are contemporary galleries all over the city, particularly in the **Jordaan** (*see p115*). In recent years, urban art pioneers have headed to Noord, where the shipyard-turned-studio complex **NDSM** (*see p160*) and other sites have become breeding grounds for creativity. The city also has a rich tradition of street art; a collection of the best and brightest is showcased at the **Street Art Museum Amsterdam** (Immanuel Kanthof 1, streetartmuseumamsterdam.com).

Brick by brick

Prime viewing time for Amsterdam's classic architecture is late on a summer's afternoon, when the sun gently picks out the varying colours and patterns of the brickwork. Then, as twilight falls, the canal houses – most of them more window than wall – light up like strings of lanterns, and you get a glimpse of the beautifully preserved, frequently opulent interiors that lie hidden behind the frontage. The best examples are to be found in the city's iconic canal district, the **Grachtengordel** (*see p95*), which was named a UNESCO World Heritage Site in 2010.

Red Light District

Then there are the *hofjes* or almshouses, hidden courtyards secluded from the city's bustle. The most famous

Sex and the City

Prostitution in Amsterdam

The recorded history of prostitution in the city dates back to the 13th century, when Amsterdam was a small fishing town. Two centuries later, it had grown into a bustling port attracting plenty of money, rich merchants and sailors, which in turn increased the amount of sex for sale. However, it wasn't only lascivious men who influenced the industry's growth, but also the fact that many local women, separated from their seafaring husbands for months on end, were left with little or no means to sustain themselves. Prostitution was one of the few money-making options available.

In the Middle Ages, the city's prostitutes were permitted to work at one of the brothels located on what is now Damstraat. Keeping a whorehouse was the exclusive privilege of Amsterdam's sheriff, and women found working elsewhere in the city were marched to the said sheriff to the 'sound of drums and flutes'. In the 15th century, however, prostitutes began working the area around Zeedijk; and by the 17th century, some were walking through the Old Side with red lanterns to advertise their profession. Soon after, enterprising women started 'advertising' themselves in the windows of their own homes or from front-facing rooms rented from other homeowners – and it's from this practice that today's more garish window trade is descended.

Working as a prostitute has been legal in Amsterdam since 1911; the women have had their own union since 1984 (De Rode Draad, or 'the Red Thread'); and prostitution was defined as a legal and taxable profession in 1988. However, it wasn't until 2000 that the ban on brothels was lifted, thus formally permitting sex work (a tactic intended to make taxation easier). With the legalisation of brothels came bureaucratisation: now, all sex workers must be in possession of an EU passport, and a 200-page rule book governs the selling of sexual services – everything from fire escapes to the appropriate length of a prostitute's fingernails.

Although the legal changes mean that sex workers have access to social services and can legitimately band together to improve their working conditions, the stigma remains. It's still difficult for prostitutes to get bank accounts, mortgages and insurance, despite being liable for taxes and generating an estimated half a billion euros a year.

In 2007, Project 1012 was launched to clean up Amsterdam's infamous Red Light District (1012 is the area's postcode) by then-deputy mayor Lodewijk Asscher. New legislation gave the city the power to withdraw property rights from those suspected of criminal activities and to buy their properties under compulsory purchase orders. Since then, almost 130 windows have been shut, despite protests from local brothel owners. However, following a march on city hall and accusations that politicians were using the sex trade as an excuse to grab valuable property, the closure of sex windows was halted at the end of 2015. Nevertheless, the impact of Project 1012 is very evident in the area and the clean-up initiative continues. Critics believe reducing the number of windows has pushed the sex industry underground where it can't be regulated – thereby making conditions for sex workers far worse.

is the **Begijnhof** (*see p90*), but there are plenty of others in the Jordaan. Entrances are sometimes locked in deference to the residents, but take a chance and you may be surprised by the delights inside.

Amsterdam's other major contribution to architecture came in the early 20th century with the Amsterdam School led by Hendrik Berlage, whose work was characterised by (often rounded) brick constructions and intricate detailing. It was used for working-class housing, schools and institutions, including **Museum Het Schip** (*see p120*). Other examples can be seen on Spaarndammerbuurt, Rivierenbuurt, Concertgebouwbuurt and the area around Mercantorplein.

Dutch architectural innovation has continued in the 21st century with the construction of sustainable housing solutions and eye-catching buildings, such as the **EYE Film Institute** (*see p154*), around the docks and waterfront. Details of these and other projects are on show at **ARCAM** – the Architectuurcentrum Museum Amsterdam (*see p154*). But the real story has been the redevelopment of the city's former industrial sites into thriving cultural hubs, including **Westergasfabriek** (*see p123*), the **A'DAM Toren** (*see p153*) and **NDSM**.

Sights unseen

Much of Amsterdam's charm derives from what remains hidden to the untutored eye. There is plenty to see in the city centre, of course: medieval buildings, the Red Light District, grand 17th-century houses, ancient churches and the oldest and prettiest canals. But be sure to venture beyond the constraints of the Grachtengordel to the newly gentrified residential areas of **De Pijp** (*see p163*) and the **Jordaan**, or further afield to **Noord** (*see p151*), to immerse yourself in the locals' Amsterdam and to discover the latest trends in cuisine and culture.

Eating & Drinking

Although Amsterdam doesn't have an especially distinguished culinary history, its restaurant scene is thriving. Tourist numbers are up, thanks to the city's reinvigorated cultural offerings, and the hotel-restaurant-café business, or *horeca*, is clearly benefitting. Its foodie movement reflects trends currently in vogue in other major cities, with Instagram-friendly pop-ups, guest chefs and sustainable fare taking centre stage, but with a uniquely Dutch spin on both international and local flavours.

The city's drinking options are also far more sophisticated than the inebriated stag-doers may have you believe. Whether you like your drinks distilled, caffeinated or heavily alcoholic, Amsterdam has a liquid offering to suit most tastes, from boutique cocktail lounges to authentic brown bars to hipster coffee outlets.

Blowout meal
Try &Samhoud Places' (p157) lavish molecular menu and visit Moon (p159), which literally revolves as you dine.

Global flavours
Blauw (p80) serves up traditional Indonesian, while indoor street food market Food Hallen (p133) offers a world of choice.

National dishes
There's Dutch food overlooking a canal at Bistro Bij Ons (p101), and home cooking at bargain prices at Hap Hmm (p133).

Cocktails with a view
Dip your feet into the infinity pool at MR PORTER (p93) and live the high life at Twenty Third Bar (p169).

Get the beers in
Brouwerij 't IJ (p148) – a brewery under a windmill. Enough said. Choose from hundreds of beers at Gollem's Proeflokaal (p136).

Traditional drinking dens
It doesn't come more old school than Café de Dokter (p93) or ancient *jenever* distillery Wynand Fockink (p83).

Netherlands on a plate

Admittedly light on culinary accolades when compared to its Western European counterparts, Amsterdam hasn't typically been a pinnacle of gastronomic glamour. But the country is fast catching up. Well-travelled native chefs have returned home to apply their skills to fresh, local and often organic ingredients (source your own at **Noordermarkt**'s Saturday organic market; *see p125*).

The land is most suited to growing spuds, cabbage, kale and carrots, but the future-focused nation is making sustainable strides with greenhouses growing a startling array of ingredients, year-round. Organic eating is well and truly trendy, thanks largely to the revival of the city's post-industrial Noord area. Here, abandoned warehouses have been converted into sustainable restaurants such as **Pllek** (*see p161*) and **Café de Ceuvel** (*see p158*), which has its own rooftop farm. Both menus only feature locally sourced organic produce.

In medieval days fish, gruel and beer formed the holy diet. During the Golden Age, the rich indulged in hogs and pheasants enlivened by spices, sugar and exotic fruits from the burgeoning Dutch Empire. The potato reigned supreme in the following centuries, until, after World War II, the rich, spicy food from Indonesia reawoke the Dutch palate. Indonesian *rijsttafel* ('rice table'), along with fondue – a 'national' dish shamelessly stolen from the Swiss because its shared pot appealed to the Dutch sense of democracy – are both foods of choice for any celebratory meals. Other waves of immigration helped create today's vortex of culinary diversity.

That said, there's still nothing quite like a hotchpotch of mashed potato, crispy bacon and crunchy greens, holding a well of gravy and loads of smoked sausage, to prove that traditional Dutch food can still hit the spot.

Where to eat

Several 'culinary boulevards' have recently staked their claim. One is located on a stretch of connected streets in the Jordaan that has become known as 'Little Italy' because of its highly regarded restaurants. Another culinary strip is Amstelveenseweg, bordering the south end of Vondelpark.

Appelkoek

In the know
Price categories

All our restaurant listings are marked with a euro symbol category, indicating the price you should expect to pay for a standard main course. The final bill will of course depend on the number of courses and drinks consumed.

€ = under €10

€€ = €10-€20

€€€ = €20-€30

€€€€ = over €30

If you enjoy a stroll that involves picking out where you're going to eat dinner, here are a few tips: go to De Pijp or Amsterdam East if you crave economical ethnic; cruise Haarlemmerstraat, Utrechtsestraat, Nieuwmarkt, the 'Nine Streets' area and Reguliersdwarsstraat if you want something more upmarket; and only surrender to Leidseplein if you don't mind being over-charged for a cardboard steak or day-old sushi.

Café or bar?

The café (or bar – the line between the two is suitably blurred) is central to Dutch social life, serving as a home from home at all hours of the day and night (most cafés open in the morning and don't shut until 1am; some stay open as late as 3am or 4am at weekends). Whatever the hour, you're as likely to find punters sipping a coffee or a cola as the foaming head of a pils – or a shot of local gin.

What to drink

Wine buffs may be underwhelmed by Amsterdam's traditional *bruin* (brown) cafés, but there are plenty of other options if you are aghast at the prospect of a beaker

Little Collins

Street Eats

From 'fat bites' to raw herring, this is the best fast food in town

Broodjes

Traditional Dutch sandwiches filled with meats and cheese are available from bakers and butchers, but you can also try more creative variations that highlight the city's multiculturalism, such as spicy Surinamese *broodjes* from Chin-Indo-Suri snack bars and rolled 'pizzas' from Turkish bakeries.

Frites

The best are the chunky Belgian ones (*Vlaamse frites*), double-fried to ensure a crispy exterior and creamy interior. Enjoy them with a topping of *oorlog* ('war'): mayo, spicy peanut sauce and onions. **Vleminckx** (*see p92*) and **Manneken Pis** (Damrak 41, near Centraal Station) are two of the best chip shops.

Haring

In Amsterdam you must – yes, you really must – try raw herring. The fish is at its best between May and July when the plump *Hollandse nieuwe* catch hits the stands and the sweet flesh can be eaten unadulterated by onions and pickles. There's a quality fish stall or shop around most corners.

Vette hap

The local term for a greasy snack translates literally as 'fat bite'. At the ubiquitous **FEBO**, you can put your change into the glowing vending machine and, in return, get a hot hamburger, *bamibal* (a deep-fried noodle ball of vaguely Indonesian descent), or a *kaas soufflé* (a cheese treat). The most popular choice – and rightly so – are *kroketten*. The Dutch answer to Spanish *croquetas*, *kroketten* are a melange of meat and potato with deep-fried skins, best served on a bun with hot mustard and washed down with a pint.

Mannekenpis

of unspecified red or white. Head to **Vyne** (*p102*) or **Bubbles & Wines** (*see p81*) – both establishments specialise in pairing good food with fine wine.

Cocktails remain ever popular, be they the ultra-posh secret concoctions made at **Hiding in Plain Sight** (*see p148*), drinks with a view at the likes of **Twenty Third Bar** (*see p169*) and **MR PORTER** (*see p93*), or boozy brunch classics at **Little Collins** (Eerste Sweelinckstraat 19, 753 9636, www.littlecollins.nl).

A barfly can score some major points by giving the Dutch their rightful credit for inventing gin. In around 1650 a doctor in Leiden came up with the process that allowed juniper berries to be infused into distilled spirits, and gin was born – or rather *jenever*, as the local version is called. A few decades later, the Dutch were exporting 10 million gallons of the stuff, as a supposedly innocuous cure for stomach and kidney ailments. They graded the gin by age – *jong*, *oud* and *zeer oud* (young, old and very old) – but also by adding various herbs, spices and flavours. Such liquid elixirs can still be found at *proeflokalen* (tasting houses) like **Wynand Fockink** (*see p83*).

Beer, though, is resoundingly the local drink of choice: in most places the pils is Heineken or Amstel, but every bar offers a range of Belgian brews and there are several specialist beer bars such as **Brouwerij 't IJ** (*see p148*). For a real taste of all the Low Countries' native brews, **'t Arendsnest** (*see p101*) has a huge range to choose from. Perhaps the most fundamental rule for Brits is not to whine about the 'two fingers' of head that comes with a glass of draft pils (lager).

Jenever in traditional tulip-shaped glasses

If caffeine is more your buzz, Amsterdam is regaining its status as a java hub. The Dutch played a fundamental role in establishing the global coffee market after a Dutchman smuggled a coffee plant out of Yemen in 1690, and sent clones to Dutch colonies in Sumatra, Java, Ceylon (now Sri Lanka) and Suriname, where they flourished.

't Smalle p124

Now, more than three centuries later, independent coffee houses are energising the city's café scene. **Lot Sixty One** supplies beans to cafés and restaurants across the city, as well as having its own sit-in corner on the Kinkerstraat (*see p133*). Over in De Pijp, **CT Coffee & Coconuts** (*see p167*) sets a high bar when it comes to caffeine, but the likes of **Scandinavian Embassy** (*see p169*), **Bakers & Roasters** (*see p166*) and **Espressofabriek** (Gosschalklaan 7, 486 2106, www.espressofabriek.nl) manage to meet it.

Where to drink

A cool yet hard-drinking kind of crowd can be found at **Café Eijlders** (*see p102*) and other cafés along Marnixstraat, just off Leidseplein. A short hop in the other direction is Reguliersdwarsstraat, the centre of both the gay scene and an emerging more mixed trendy scene as exemplified by **Taboo Bar** (Reguliersdwarsstraat 45, www.taboobar.nl). And one of Amsterdam's best mixed gay bars, **Prik** (*see p94*), which serves everyone's favourite bubbly – prosecco – on tap, is but a ten-minute walk away.

Away from the neon, the Jordaan is awash with brown cafés. You can spot them on most street corners but for a story you'll tell for years head to **Café Nol** (*see p122*), probably the best-known bar in the neighbourhood. Not far away stands the **Westergasfabriek** (*see p123*), which has several appealing drinking spots, including the WestergasTerras. A similar scene to the Jordaan is to be found in De Pijp, a great place to wander between trendy bars and more salt-of-the-earth watering holes. To soak up the city's most impressive revival, head across the IJ to **Noord** for drinks with a view of the city.

Amsterdam's Coffeeshops

More than just coffee ...

Each coffeeshop has a different ambience, but all are bound by strict regulations: licensed premises must display a white and green sticker; they can only sell five grams of cannabis to each customer per day; they are not permitted to sell alcohol, and they are banned from advertising (so if a coffeeshop has a website at all, it will be a 'fan site'). Under-18s are not permitted to enter a coffeeshop.

What's on offer

Smoking tobacco is not allowed in public spaces in the Netherlands (including, perversely, coffeeshops), so you can only smoke 'pure' weed, although many shops have sealed rooms for tobacco smoking, or may offer bongs, vapourisers or herbal mixes as alternatives. Others sell spacecakes and hash brownies; be very careful if you choose to indulge in these edible forms of the drug however, as the effects can take a while to kick in and may be very intense. Magic mushrooms are no longer legal.

When you first walk in, ask to see a menu: it will list the available drugs and their prices. Seek the advice of the staff, who can explain the effects of each option and give you a look and a smell. Prices vary: expect to pay an average of €8 for a gram, but prices can go up to around €40, depending on quality. Coffeeshops in the centre tend to be more expensive than those in outlying districts.

Hash is typically named after its country of origin (Moroccan, Afghan, Lebanese), whereas weed usually bears invented names loosely referring to an element of the strain (White Widow, Super Skunk, Silver Haze). Beware homegrown Dutch weed, which is notoriously strong, containing more than 15 per cent of the intoxicating THC (tetrahydrocannabinol), and should be avoided. (There have been moves to reclassify such strains as 'hard drugs', with accompanying stiff penalties.)

All shops provide free rolling papers and tips, and if you're in a hurry, pre-rolled joints are always available; these usually contain low-grade ingredients, although a few shops pride themselves on excellent pre-rolls.

Shopping

Amsterdam's shopping scene has come a long way since the 'tulip mania' of the 17th-century Golden Age, when single bulbs were traded for cash, castles and mountains of cheese (though the latter is still a crowd favourite). Today, the city is flanked by an array of stores as interesting as the people wandering its streets. From the tacky neon-lit tourist digs in the Red Light District to the high-end boutiques along PC Hoofstraat, the city's shops will cater to just about any buyer or budget.

The buoyancy of the retail sector could be explained by the simple fact that the Netherlands is a relatively wealthy country. Yet while the Dutch clearly spend, the population is perhaps less obsessed with shopping than residents of other countries. The influence of Calvinism, that most pared-down of lifestyle choices, is still etched deep into the national psyche.

Unique souvenirs
Gilian Originals (*p111*) has handmade jewellery and there are quirky gifts from Otherist (*p104*).

Bustling markets
Hunt for bargains at Albert Cuypmarkt (*p168*) and Noord's Pekmarkt (*p162*).

High design
Blom & Blom (*p162*) and Hôtel Droog (*p84*) offer ingenious designs for home, garden and beyond.

Original fashion
Go back in time at Bij Ons Vintage (*p94*), and visit Hester van Eeghen (*p104*) for Dutch designer footwear.

One-stop shopping
Don't miss Hutspot Amsterdam (*p170*) – a whole store of pop-ups – and hip Nine Streets (*p103*).

Books
Bag antique books at the Spui's Friday book market (*p94*) and at Oudemanhuis Book Market (*p84*).

Markets

Tulips are perhaps what Amsterdam is best known for exporting, and you can certainly pick up bargains at the floating flower market **Bloemenmarkt** (*see p111*). At more traditional general markets, you'll find people bouncing between vendors, sniffing out special offers.

People from all walks of life are brought together at the **Albert Cuypmarkt** (*see p168*), which claims to be Europe's longest street market, and forms a line through the heart of De Pijp. The daily market offers plenty of snacks, ranging from raw herrings to Surinamese sherbets, along with all manner of household goods.

Other neighbourhoods in the city have their own markets: **Pekmarkt** (*see p162*) in Noord and the **Dappermarkt** in Oost are all worth a trip. Also located in the Jordaan, Saturday's **Noordermarkt** is the place to buy organic farmers' produce amid well-heeled shoppers; the same crowd is back on Monday morning to pick through bric-a-brac and antiques, at a smaller (but superior) variation on Waterlooplein's touristy **flea market** (*see p149*).

Bloemenmarkt

Fashion

The Dutch haven't traditionally had the best reputation for fashion but the city's creative types and young blood are transforming the stereotype with style. If you wander through the city's streets or people-watch from a canalside café, you'll notice that the Dutch favour a casual-chic look. Trainers are paired with just about any outfit and a 'less is more' approach makes for a simplistic and timeless style.

A fair few designers have also achieved success in Amsterdam, and the country can hold its head high in the catwalk stakes – after all, it's the home city of avant-garde darlings Viktor & Rolf and ever-charming Marlies Dekkers, with her feminine lingerie. A couple of Dutch brands have brought street style home: Gsus and G-Star Raw. Affordable high-end wear from Scotch & Soda is also doing its part to put the spotlight on Amsterdam.

The city's fashion map is divided along clear lines: head to PC Hooftstraat, as star footballers do, for designer clothes; visit the Kalverstraat for high-street stalwarts such as H&M and HEMA. Even though Amsterdam has long lacked an abundance of good boutiques, a wander around the Jordaan, the Nine Streets and Damstraat areas will lead to the discovery of outlets selling quirkier and home-grown labels.

For something trendy, De Pijp certainly delivers, with eclectic boutique offering at **Anna + Nina** (*see p170*) and permanent pop-up department store, **Hutspot** (*see p170*), which sells coffee and art alongside its clothing.

Interior design and homewares

Sneak a peek into just about any Amsterdam home and the city's interior design prowess will become apparent. To feed your eyes with design of all kinds, from seriously high-end homeware to truly swanky jewellery, check out **Utrechtsestraat**. Overtoom, Rozengracht and Haarlemmerstraat/ Haarlemmerdijk are also the destinations of much-coveted furnishings.

Waterlooplein flea market

Where to Spend it

Amsterdam's shopping districts – the cheat sheet

Damstraat

A street at war with its former self, Damstraat is a rather eclectic mix of predictable tourist tackiness and trendy unassuming boutiques. Be warned, its proximity to the Red Light District means that the countless laddish types out on the town can impinge on this otherwise lovely area.

Haarlemmerstraat & Haarlemmerdijk

Forming the northern border of Western Canal Belt and the Jordaan, these connected streets have bloomed into a remarkable culinary/boutique destination.

Jordaan

Tiny backstreets laced with twisting canals, cosy boutiques, lush markets, bakeries, galleries, restful old-fashioned cafés and bars. The Jordaan captures the spirit of Amsterdam like nowhere else in the city. The 'hood is also handily cut in half by furnishings- and design-rich street Rozengracht.

Kalverstraat & Nieuwendijk

Kalverstraat and its scruffier extension Nieuwendijk are where the locals come for their consumer kicks. Shops here are ones you'll recognise – mainly high-street stores – and they get insanely busy at weekends. Still, it's pedestrian-only, so you can forget the dreaded bikes and focus on the tills; just make sure you follow the unwritten law of keeping to the left as you cruise up or down the street.

Leidsestraat

Connecting Koningsplein and Leidseplein, Leidsestraat is peppered with fine shoe shops and more high-street shops, but you'll still have to dodge trams to shop there. Cyclists: note that bikes aren't allowed along this strip.

Magna Plaza

Right behind Dam Square, this architectural treat was once a post office. Its subsequent reincarnation as a five-floor mall is beloved by tourists, although the locals are somewhat less keen.

Nine Streets

The small streets connecting Prinsengracht, Keizersgracht and Herengracht in between Raadhuisstraat and Leidsegracht offer a very diverse mix of boutiques, antiques shops and a good range of quirky speciality stores (see p103 Nine Streets).

PC Hooftstraat

Amsterdam's elite shopping strip is undeniably high-end and expensive. Its designer shops embrace both established and up-and-coming names. Come here for the world's biggest luxury brands and to see how the other half live.

De Pijp

This bustling district is notable mainly for the Albert Cuypmarkt and its ethnic food shops, but more fashion boutiques are filling the continually gentrifying gaps.

Spiegelkwartier

Across from the Rijksmuseum and centred on Spiegelgracht, this area is packed with antiques shops selling real treasures at suitably high prices. Dress for success and keep your nose in the air if you want to fit in with the big-spending locals here.

Open books

The Dutch are incredibly bookish, so if you're a bookworm, you'll be in good company. Head straight to Spui, to be greeted by the **Friday book market**. Another singular browsing experience awaits if you cross the Rokin to reach Oudemanhuispoort, a covered passageway belonging to the University of Amsterdam where books and prints have been sold since the 18th century.

Incredible edibles

If you're hoping to pick up edible souvenirs, you'll be spoilt for choice; head to **De Kaaskamer** (Runstraat 7, 623 3483, www.kaaskamer.nl) and you'll see a mountain of cheese – there are more than 200 varieties, including plenty of local specialities such as the popular *reypenaer*. For fishy dishes, you can pick up smoked eel, raw herring or tiny North Sea shrimps from any number of fish stalls dotted around town. Head to **Patisserie Holtkamp**

De Kaaskamer

(Vijzelgracht 15, 624 8757) for an array of cakes displayed in a beautiful interior; you will also be able to see how this gourmet shop cooks the humble *kroket*. If you fancy locally produced, organic food, visit **Marqt** (Overtoom 21, 820 8292, www.marqt. com) – if it happens to have lamb from the North Sea island of Texel, or white asparagus, make sure you try some.

Entertainment

Amsterdam likes to see itself as a major hub in the cultural universe. Locals give standing ovations to Beethoven symphonies, lap up the latest operas from Pierre Audi or Dmitri Tcherniakov, and also dance for three days straight to DJs like Tiesto and Martin Garrix.

The city has more than its fair share of world-class venues for every form of cultural endeavour. Add to this an active underground art and club scene, and visitors are spoilt for choice. The breadth and quality of the Amsterdam arts experience was long due to enlightened funding from government and city council alike, resulting in a wealth of arts festivals, plus buildings such as the Muziekgebouw. However, more recent subsidy cutbacks have forced larger companies to merge and smaller initiatives to fight for their existence. Clubs and live music venues, however, have been given a boost in the form of a nachtburgemeester (night mayor) Mirik Milan, who has campaigned for 24-hour licences.

❤ Shortlist

Silver screen
The futuristic EYE Film Institute (*p154*) and art deco wonder, Pathé Tuschinski (*p114*).

Concert halls
The acoustically blessed Concertgebouw (*p140*) and Muziekgebouw (*p162*).

Dance until dawn
Get your EDM fix 24 hours a day at De School (*p126*) and Shelter (*p162*).

Contemporary kicks
Weird and wonderful mixed media offerings at NDSM (*p160*) and Westergasfabriek (*p123*).

High culture
Nationale Opera & Ballet (*p150*) for dance and opera, and the palatial Stadsschouwburg (*p106*).

Jazz joints
The cosy but classy Bourbon Street (*p112*) and North Sea Jazz Club (*p126*).

Live music
Melkweg (*p105*) and Paradiso (*p113*) for big bands on a small scale.

LGBT clubs
Anything goes at Club Church (*p112*). For attitude-free fun, opt for Prik (*p94*).

Classical music

One of the most heart-warming aspects of Amsterdam's cultural scene is that the city promotes a classless adoration of beautiful music. Attending a concert is not a grand statement of one's arrival in society; it's simply about love of the music. Many of the greatest international orchestras perform in Amsterdam – typically for little more than the price of the biggest rock or pop concerts, and frequently for considerably less. The city is also home to world-renowned orchestras and soloists, and renditions of the classics are not limited to the grand concert venues, but can be heard alongside canals, in parks, on the streets or in the halls of the Conservatorium van Amsterdam building – whose composers-in-training are being brought to the fore thanks to the likes of the new-music specialist **Asko-Schönberg Ensemble** (www.askoschoenberg.nl). Dutch composer and pianist Louis Andriessen is also on the global radar, having been awarded the prestigious

Muziekgebouw

Marie-Josée Kravis Prize for New Music by the New York Philharmonic in 2016.

The renowned **Royal Concertgebouw Orchestra** (www.concertgebouworkest.nl), led by chief conductor Daniele Gatti, plays at the acoustically blessed Concertgebouw for most of the season (which kicks off in September); try to hear them, if possible, even if just for a lunchtime concert. The German conductor Marc Albrecht, meanwhile, leads the **Dutch National Opera**, the **Netherlands Philharmonic Orchestra** and the **Netherlands Chamber Orchestra** (www.orkest.nl).

Clubbing

Amsterdam's electronic dance music (EDM) scene has long been acknowledged as one of the best in the world, and not just for its homegrown-turned-global talents, including Martin Garrix and DJ Isis among others. The annual Amsterdam Dance Event attracted a record-breaking 375,000 visitors in 2016, and in 2015, ING estimated the Netherlands' EDM industry to be worth €200 million. Although infamous dance clubs Trouw Amsterdam and Studio 80 have called it a night for good, pioneers of Amsterdam's ever-evolving club scene were quick to replace them with the likes of **De School** (*see p126*) and **Shelter** (*see p162*), a dance music haven in the basement of Noord's **A'DAM Toren** (*see p153*). Both of these have been granted the insatiable club-goer's golden ticket: 24-hour licensing (*see p46* Amsterdam After Dark.

The city's club offering is dance-heavy, but diversification is still apparent. Hip hop and R&B reign supreme at the likes of **Jimmy Woo** (*see p105*), while globally renowned venues **Paradiso** (*see p113*) and **Melkweg** (*see p105*) play host to an eclectic mix of pop, dance and alternative artists in the international spotlight.

There are scuzzy venues for students and rockers, meat markets for stags, and cutting-edge clubs for hipsters. Note that concerts at rock, pop and jazz venues often run into club nights.

In recent years, the festival scene has absolutely exploded countrywide, with the emergence of crowd-pleasing boutique dance festivals such as 18hrs Festival and Pitch. As after-dark innovators make use of the city's post-industrial warehouse spaces, such as **Pllek** (*see p161*) and **NDSM** (*see p160*), it seems likely that this trend is likely to continue for many moons to come.

Dance

Schizophrenic is probably the best way to describe Dutch dance. On the one hand, it has a boutique, experimental feel, with outlandish domestic creations that are hard on both eye and ear. On the other, its two

In the know
Top tickets

Tickets for most performances can be bought at the venues or via their websites. If playing it by ear, try the Last Minute Ticket Shop (www.lastminuteticketshop.nl), where tickets for that night are sold at half price from 10am local time. You can also buy tickets from Ticketmaster (www.ticketmaster.nl).

Where the Art is

The city that is defined by its creativity

Amsterdam is home to some of the most instantly recognisable works in history, but art-lovers are lured by far more than Rembrandts, Van Goghs and Vermeers. Critics have hailed the city's surge in contemporary art as something of an artistic renaissance.

Perhaps it's because Amsterdam has embraced new media like few other cities. The pioneering **Waag Society** (www.waag.org) and the happily subversive **Mediamatic** (www.mediamatic.net) both arose from the 'tactical media' scene. Mediamatic explores both the possibilities and challenges technology offers art, with lectures on sustainable food and an on-site aquaponics greenhouse.

Photography, too, has found a place in the city psyche. It has often been said that Amsterdam, with its soggy climate and bleak winters, was designed to look as good in black and white as it does in colour, making it especially appealing to amateur snappers.

The city is a strong supporter of the photographic arts, with **Foam** (see p110) providing solid institutional backing.

What makes Amsterdam such a hotbed for creativity in the 21st century? One simple answer might be: money. The cost of living is far lower here than other urban hubs such as London and New York. Historically, the Dutch government has been generous with subsidies for artists. As the home of prestigious art residency the **Rijksakademie** (www.rijksakademie.nl) and acclaimed art/design university **Gerrit Rietveld Academie** (www. gerritrietveldacademie. nl), Amsterdam is teeming with young, up-and-coming artists from all over the world, who are producing work, in all media, like crazy. This international influence helps explain why the city's galleries are more adventurous and welcoming to young artists and curators than elsewhere.

headline companies, the Dutch National Ballet (based in Amsterdam) and the Nederlands Dans Theater (based in the Hague), are the envy of the international classical and contemporary dance worlds. Foreign choreographers, such as Jirí Kylián, Krzysztof Pastor, William Forsythe, Wayne Eagling and Lightfoot León, have also seen their works flourish with regular premieres at the city's most important venues, the **Stadsschouwburg** (*see p106*) and **Nationale Opera & Ballet** (*see p150*). Commercial fare passes through the **Amsterdam RAI Theater** (Europaplein 2, 549 1212, www.rai.nl), care of the Kirov and Bolshoi Russian ballet companies, while the less classically minded should pay a visit to the city in July, when the Leidseplein theatres host **Julidans** (www.julidans.nl), a festival for the very latest international dance styles.

Film

The Dutch are not major global players when it comes to film. Reported industry figures from 2016 put the country's share of the film market at an all-time low, with only ten per cent of cinema revenue from Dutch-made films. But the country is not without its share of creative talent. Dutch director Paul Verhoeven, best known for blockbuster flicks *Robocop* and *Basic Instinct*, was selected to head up the jury at the Berlin International Film Festival in 2017. You may also recognise Dutch household names such as *Game of Thrones* actress Carice van Houten and *Control* director Anton Corbijn. And then there are the transplants, such as directors Steve McQueen (*12 Years a Slave*) and Peter Greenaway (*Nightwatching*).

> ### In the know
> **Access all areas**
>
> A fictional town called Cineville (www.cineville.nl) brings together 16 arthouse and repertory cinemas in Amsterdam, including EYE and FilmHallen, and more than 20 cinemas across the country. A pass costing €19 a month provides access to them all.

The city is home to some of Europe's most beautiful mainstream cinemas (including art deco delight **Pathé Tuschinski**, *see p114*), a fine crop of arthouse institutions, film festivals aplenty and the brilliant film institute **EYE** (*see p154*), reaching for the celluloid stars.

LGBT

Amsterdam's standing as a 'gay capital' seemed to be on the slide in the decade after it held the world's first same sex wedding in 2001, but playing host to EuroPride in 2016 reaffirmed the city's place on the LGBT map. Today,

Amsterdam remains keen to broadcast its credentials as a haven for liberalism and open-mindedness. It has an impressive track record when it comes to gay rights: homosexuality was decriminalised in 1811, the first gay/lesbian bar opened in 1927 (Café 't Mandje, still open today), and one of the first gay rights organisations, COC Nederland, was founded in Amsterdam in 1946, at a time when much of the rest of the world considered homosexuality an illness. Local political parties have tried hard to make Amsterdam gay-friendly and, in 2016, King Willem-Alexander visited COC Nederland to help celebrate the 70th anniversary of the gay liberation movement.

Until recently, the scenes for gay men and women were quite separate and they'd only get together on big occasions such as King's Day, Pride or one-off parties like

Amsterdam After Dark

The 24-hour city that knows how to party

'Multi-disciplinary, high quality and long lasting' is how Amsterdam's *nachtburgemeester* (night mayor), Mirik Milan, describes the city's offering when the sun goes down. Once typecast by tales of debauchery and crude excess, the city's nocturnal scene is now mentioned in the same breath as New York, London and Berlin, despite being a fraction of their size. Whether it's for the stereotypical-red light-centred stag do or to dance for three days straight, Amsterdam's nightlife is a major draw for the millions who visit each year.

Milan has been nurturing the city's after-dark scene since 2012, when he was elected to what was then a voluntary post to help rebuild communication between the nocturnal souls and daytime politicians. At the time, Amsterdam nightlife was gradually awakening from a regulation-induced slumber. Locals had complained for years that nightlife was dead, after city by-laws forced clubs and pubs to close early, and underground parties were vigorously monitored and shut. After much lobbying, nine drinking and dining zones were given 24-hour licences; five of these are nightclubs. By 2014, Milan's role was more than just a cool title – it became a paid position dedicated to improving the economic and cultural value of the night across all fronts, without alienating residents and public officials. Tough gig, but improve it did.

The *nachtburgemeester*'s approach of nurturing the night as an engine for cultural and economic growth is proving so successful that other cities are following suit. Amsterdam hosted the first ever Night Mayor Summit in 2016, and the model has now been adopted by London, Toulouse, Paris and Zurich. One initiative that seems to have enjoyed particular success is a pilot system called Square Hosts, which sees 20 trained 'hosts' patrolling Rembrandtplein between 9pm and 6am every Friday and Saturday, with the aim of making everyone feel safe and welcome. The hosts are paid for by the clubs in return for longer opening hours.

As a result of Milan's efforts, Amsterdam was dubbed the nightlife capital of Europe in 2016. While the city is best known for its electronic dance scene, its cultural offering is gradually diversifying to cater for a global audience, and the live music scene, while smaller than in some other cities, is going from strength to strength.

Gay Pride

the mighty Love Dance. During recent years, however, the number of mixed bars and club nights has increased (although strictly lesbian events are still relatively few). The gay clubbing scene is thriving, reinvigorated by fresh faces such as cruising club **Church** (*see p112*).

    Amsterdam Gay Pride (*see p62*) has gone the way of many other Gay Prides worldwide by embracing corporate sponsorship – some major companies and banks even have their own floats to make sure spectators get the message (the main message being that they're keen to emphasise their employee diversity).

Theatre

Even the flying visitor to Amsterdam will recognise it as a city of art and artists. Less evident, however, is its active and passionate theatre scene, which tends to thrive in secret back-alley venues. As you might expect from this famously open-minded city, performing artists in Amsterdam are allowed – indeed encouraged – to experiment. Experimentation happens across all forms and genres, and the results are worth investigation, so be sure to hunt out smaller, alternative venues and off-centre cultural hubs. For the bleeding edge of cutting-edge theatre, check out the absurdist multimedia works of **Pips:lab** (www.pipslab.org).

Public subsidy of the arts has come under threat in the Netherlands, as elsewhere. Witness **DeLaMar Theater** (*see p105*), situated near Leidseplein, which programmes mostly Dutch-language theatre, cabaret and musicals. Only a few years old, it was basically a €60 million gift from the VandenEnde Foundation, a cultural fund set up by insanely wealthy international theatre producer Joop van den Ende to support cultural activities in the Netherlands; other beneficiaries include photography museum **Foam** (*see p110*) and the **Stedelijk Museum** (*see p134*).

The language gap is often surprisingly well bridged by surtitles, audience interaction and strong visuals. If language is a barrier, then the multipurpose, multimedia **De Balie** (Kleine-Gartmanplantsoen 10, 553 5151, www.debalie.nl) is worth checking out. Alternatively, NDSM mounts regular site-specific pieces that transcend linguistic limitations and the multi-venue **Westergasfabriek** (*see p123*) combines live performances with other visual and creative art.

DeLaMar Theater

Amsterdam
Day by Day

King's Day

Blauwe Theehuis

Itineraries

There's more to Amsterdam than the Red Light District and Rembrandts. Whether you visit for a weekend or longer, for hedonism or high culture, there's a whole world of things to see and do in the Dutch capital – whatever your budget. Don't spend your day in a coffeeshop daze; expand your mind and horizons with a tailored tour of the city. Chose from Essential Weekend, Budget Break, Family Day Out or Active Explorer, or pick and chose elements from each to suit your own itinerary.

▶ *Budgets include transport, meals and admission prices, but not accommodation or shopping.*

ESSENTIAL WEEKEND

Amsterdam in two days

Budget €200-€250 per person
Getting around Cycling, walking, tram

DAY 1

Morning

Start the morning on two wheels like a true Amsterdammer. Rent a bike from, for example, **StarBikes** (*see p181*), just east of Centraal Station. Its rental supply is always high and its coffee is always hot. Naturally, you've pre-booked a ticket online for the **Van Gogh Museum** (*see p137*) or **Rijksmuseum** (*see p130*), so you can skip the queues. Cycle there via art and antique gallery streets Nieuwe Spiegelstraat and Spiegelgracht. If pushed for time, head straight for Floor 2 in the Rijksmuseum for the Gallery of Honour and its masterpieces. Alternatively, there are more than 700 pieces of art on display at the Van Gogh Museum.

Lunch

When you've had your fill of culture, pedal through the affluent **Museum Quarter** towards the city's green space – **Vondelpark** (*see p138*). Treat yourself to lunch with a view in the flying saucer-shaped **Blauwe Theehuis** (*see p135*) right in the middle of the park itself.

Afternoon

Head back north via the quirky retail offerings of the **Nine Streets** (*see p103*), a series of side streets connecting the three main canals of the UNESCO-listed Grachtengordel. From there it's just a short pedal past Westerkerk to the **Anne Frank Huis** (*see p100*) – again, you've really been on the ball and pre-booked a ticket online. If you need to return your bike, go via the 350-year-old distillery **Wynand Fockink** (*see p83*) for a shot or two of *jenever*, the original gin. Opt for a *kopstoot* ('head butt'), which pairs the shot with a beer.

Evening

From StarBikes, stroll through the Old Centre past the **Oude Kerk** (*see p75*) and the **Royal Palace** (*see p87*) to catch sunset from the roof terrace of **MR PORTER** (*see p93*). You don't need a reservation for a drink, just head on up to the sixth floor for a view of the skyline you won't forget. If the tapas menu doesn't take your fancy, head down Spuistraat to fuel up at **Haesje Claes** (*see p92*) before catching that excellent gig likely to be happening at **Paradiso** (*see p113*) or the **Melkweg** (*see p105*).

MR PORTER

DAY 2

Morning

You've earned a big breakfast after all the exploring yesterday. Head to trendy neighbourhood **De Pijp** for brunch at the art deco **CT Coffee & Coconuts** (*see p167*). Walk off your meal with a stroll down **Albert Cuypmarkt** (*see p68*), Monday to Saturday, or **Sarphatipark** (*see p165*) if it's a Sunday, before jumping on tram 16 towards the city centre. Get off at Spui and absorb the city's living history at **Amsterdam Museum** (*see p88*).

Lunch

Feeling peckish? Chug back a herring at the fish stall on the left of Spui Square before exploring the ancient hidden courtyard, **Begijnhof** (*see p90*).

Afternoon

If you have time to kill, the authentic and inspired works at the nearby **Original Dampkring Gallery** (Singel 395, 354 6783, odgallery.com) will set your imagination free. Just make sure you leave enough time to get to the **Amsterdam Boat Centre** (*see p98*), a two-minute walk up Singel, for your Classic Canal Cruise, which you've already pre-booked online, of course. Once you're back on dry land, take a short walk through Spui to jump on tram 14 from Amsterdam Rokin to Pontanusstraat in the Oost and walk across the bridge to enjoy some locally brewed beer in the shadow of a windmill on the packed terrace of **Brouwerij 't IJ** (*see p148*). Afterwards, walk back towards town through stunning park **Artis**, home to the city's 19th-century zoo (*see p144*). When you're ready, jump on tram 10 or 14 towards Leidseplein.

Evening

What better way to conclude your visit than with dinner and a show? Enjoy traditional Dutch fare at the 60-year-old **Hap Hmm** (*see p133*) before sinking your teeth into the cultural offering at **Stadsschouwburg**, the country's grand House of Theatre (*see p106*). Home to Toneelgroep Amsterdam, the largest theatre company in the Netherlands, this historic building provides a stage for both burgeoning theatrical talent and world-class performers. If you don't like what they're showing, you can always pop across to the **DeLaMar Theater** (*see p105*) to be delighted by whichever musical, cabaret or play it has on offer.

Stadsschouwburg

BUDGET BREAK

For the euro-conscious visitor
Budget €30-€40 per person
Getting around Walking, plus one tram ride, return ferry

Morning

Nab a complimentary coffee at various branches of **Albert Heijn** to set you up to explore the bustling **Noordermarkt** (*see p125*) in the Jordaan. On Saturdays, the whole square is taken over by organic food and vibrant shopping stalls. If you happen to visit on a Monday, you may be able to bag a bargain at the weekly flea market. Afterwards, take time to explore the area's almshouses, or *hofjes*. These charming courtyards, surrounded and concealed by higgledy-piggledy houses, were largely inhabited by widows and single women who could not afford housing in the Middle Ages.

Lunch

The big museums may cost around €17 for an adult ticket, but there are plenty of smaller galleries where it's possible to browse art for free in the **Jordaan**. Get your fill of the city's contemporary art scene before grabbing a cheap sandwich (or *broodje*) at **Comestibles Kinders** (*see p120*).

EYE Film Institute

Afternoon

Catch tram 10 to the lively Museumplein public space, bordered by the **Rijksmuseum** (*see p130*) and **Van Gogh Museum** (*see p137*). Wander through the Rijksmuseum's cavernous bicycle passage, which is a spectacle in itself with high ceilings and stunning architecture by Cruz y Ortiz. The museum has a free garden open to the public year round. During summer, the greenery is the setting for an annual sculpture display. From Museumplein, make your way towards the Old Centre via the **Woonboat Museum** (*seep101*) which offers an insight into life on the water. Saunter through the Old Centre as far as Centraal Station to catch a free ferry to Noord. Enjoy the views and then have a drink and rest your feet

at **Tolhuistuin** (*see p157*). Walk along IJ promenade to see the futuristic architecture of the **EYE Film Institute** (*see p154*) up close – in the basement there's a permanent free interactive exhibition worth checking out.

Evening

Returning to Centraal Station on the ferry, head for public library **Openbare Bibliotheek Amsterdam** (OBA, *see p157*), to flick through the international papers and glossies. Try dinner at rustic hideaway **Hannekes Boom** (*seep161*) – the restaurant on the water is good value and there's often live music and DJs playing. If energy reserves are still high, then the full-on sights, sounds and smells of the **Red Light District** make it perfect for a late-night wander.

FAMILY DAY OUT

Keeping the kids amused
Budget €250-€300 for a family of four
Getting around Canal boat, walking, trams, return ferry

Morning

Start your day at the **Hollandsche Manege** riding school in Amsterdam's **Vondelpark** (*see p138*), by catching tram 1 from Centraal Station. Enjoy a coffee while watching the horses, before taking a stroll through Vondelpark to the over-sized Iamsterdam letters in **Museumplein** (*see p127*) for a photo opportunity little ones will love.

Lunch

Take your pick from the many food stalls lining Museumplein for a cheap and easy bite to eat. For something authentically Amsterdam, grab a serving or two of *bitterballen* for the family to share. If it's a sunny day, enjoy a family picnic on the grass or by the fountains near the **Rijksmuseum** (*see p130*), which offers guided family tours should you wish to venture inside.

Rijksmuseum

If you're visiting November to February, the winter ice-skating rink is a wonderful way to keep kids occupied.

Afternoon

After re-energising at lunch, explore the city's **Grachtengordel**. Take a 10-15 minute walk (or jump on tram 16 from near the Stedelijk Museum) to board a 'Kidscruise' with the **Blue Boat Company** (*see p98*) from Stadhouderskade. Adults get a grown-up set of headphones while the kids are taken on an adventure by Johnny the mouse. Afterwards, take tram 16 to the **NEMO Science Center** (*see p156*) on Amsterdam's waterfront. Featuring a hands-on laboratory and a 'Maker Space', the museum is dedicated to blowing minds.

Evening

Walk along the waterfront back to Centraal Station, and take the brood for a bite to eat at **Sea Palace** (626 4777, seapalace. nl), where you can enjoy uninterrupted views of the IJ and Old Centre. Then, depending on the age of your offspring, either take them to a puppet show at the **Marionetten Theater** (*see p85*) or treat yourself to some much-deserved alone time with the help of a babysitting service, such as **Kriterion** (624 5848, www.oppascentralekriterion.nl). Register online and apply for a babysitter at the time and location you desire.

ACTIVE EXPLORER

Sightseeing for fitness freaks
Budget €100-€150 per person
Getting around Walking, cycling, canal bike, return ferry

Morning

Rise and shine! It's going to be a busy day. Grab a rental bike from **MacBike** in Oud West (*see p181*) then fuel up with a juice from **Marqt** (Overtoom 21, www.marqt.com), where you can pump up your tyres while you're at it. Cycle along the scenic Singelgracht to the western edge of the city and marvel at the city's former gasworks, **Westergasfabriek** (*see p123*). The buzzing urban hub is now an award-winning cultural park complete with restaurants, music venues and plenty of green space to run around. After you've rested your legs, jump back on those wheels and take the scenic route to Centraal Station via Westerdok and the **Westelijke Eilanden** near the Jordaan, for a taste of life during the Golden Age.

Lunch

When you reach Centraal, walk your bike onto one of the regular ferries to the newly revived Noord district. On reaching dry land, cycle to the **A'DAM Toren** (*see p153*). Adrenalin junkies should head to the top of the tower to A'DAM Lookout's 'Over the Edge' – Europe's highest swing, 100m (328ft) above ground. To bring your heart rate back to normal, have a restful lunch at post-industrial paradise **Pllek** (*see p161*). Consisting of shipping containers and recyclable materials, it uses mostly locally sourced and organic produce. If it's a warm day, enjoy your meal on one of the outdoor beach chairs with a picture-perfect view of the city across the water before jumping back on the return ferry towards Centraal.

Over the Edge, A'DAM Toren

Afternoon

It's almost time to return your bike, so take the scenic route back through the gorgeous **Jordaan** district. The charming streets are riddled with quirky cafés, galleries and old buildings. Once you've dropped your bike back, enjoy views of the affluent Museum Quarter as you walk the short distance to hire a canal bike from **Stromma** (Stadhouderskade 520, www.stromma.nl). Each pedalo seats four; they can be hired for up to 90 minutes and returned to various points along the Prinsengracht or Singelgracht. Just make sure you tell the staff where you are going to collect your €20 deposit.

Evening

You've certainly worked up an appetite. Fancy a meal peppered with gentle exercise and a side of entertainment? A tour with **Walking Dinner Amsterdam** (626 0016, www.puuramsterdam. nl) through the Old Centre and Red Light District ought to do the trick. Each course is enjoyed at a different restaurant and a knowledgeable guide will feed you fun facts about the city's history along the way. Dessert has never been so guilt free! If you've still got energy afterwards, burn it off at dance palace **Disco Dolly** (*see p94*). It's open every night of the week.

Diary

The Dutch have a reputation for being a fairly reserved bunch, but when they shed their inhibitions and dive into a fun-seeking frenzy, they dive deep. On the likes of Oudejaarsavond (New Year's Eve) and Koningsdag (King's Day) – or whenever AFC Ajax wins a big game – the city falls into a joyous, orange-tinted psychosis of song, drink and dance. Happily, orange is yet to play a leading role during FashionWeek (but that's not to say it won't become the new black next year).

Dance music is a big deal in Amsterdam, and its annual electronic music festivals, including Amsterdam Dance Event, are a major draw. If you prefer your culture more genteel however, there's plenty more to choose from, including Open Monument Days, the ever-popular Museum Night and even National Windmill Day.

Spring

The sun is out, blue skies are abundant and Holland's iconic tulips are popping up to say hello. Many would say that spring is the best season of the year to visit Amsterdam: the winter frost is receding and the city's beauty is more vibrant than ever. And because you're avoiding the summer crowds, you can relax and enjoy it. The Dutch don't waste any time awakening from the cold spell – they spring into the season with a host of events and activities.

Mar & Sept Amsterdam Restaurant Week
www.restaurantweek.nl
Book online fast to secure a three-course gourmet dinner in a top restaurant for only €27.50.

Early Mar Roze Filmdagen
www.rozefilmdagen.nl
Literally Amsterdam's 'pink film days'; a ten-day showcase of queer-minded flicks from around the world, at Westergasfabriek (*see p123*).

Mid Mar Cinedans
www.cinedans.nl
International dance and movie festival at the EYE Film Institute (*see p154*).

Mid Mar Stille Omgang
www.stille-omgang.nl
The candlelit Silent Procession commemorates the 14th-century Miracle of Amsterdam through the night, around the Old Centre.

Early Apr Tulip Festival
www.tulpfestival.com
Amsterdam celebrates its beloved tulip with a display of over 500,000 of the most colourful and rare specimens throughout the city.

Early-mid Apr National Museum Weekend
www.museumweekend.nl
The country's 500 or so state-funded museums offer free or discounted admission and special activities for this one weekend.

Mid Apr Imagine Film Festival
www.imaginefilmfestival.nl
Festival offering films for gorehounds and those with a predilection for fantasy and sci-fi.

Mid Apr-July World Press Photo
www.worldpressphoto.org
The world's largest photography competition kicks off in the Nieuwe Kerk (*see p89*), then tours another 100 locations around the world.

♥ 27 Apr Koningsdag (King's Day)
The most popular event in the city starts the night before, with street parties and late-night drinking sessions in cafés. By day, the canals become a sea of orange as they are overrun with party boats and floats. Party-lovers and students of the surreal should make sure their visit coincides with this date, when up to a million extra people pour into the city. With sound systems galore in the streets and on the water, it's all quite insane.

Tulips

4 & 5 May **Herdenkingsdag & Bevrijdingsdag**

At 7.30pm on 4 May, those who died in World War II are remembered at the Nationaal Monument. Liberation Day (to mark the end of Nazi occupation) is celebrated the next day with music and speeches.

Early May-early Sept **Vondelpark Openluchttheater**

www.openluchttheater.nl
The open-air stage in Vondelpark is used to the max, with a free programme that ranges from classical music to stand-up to pop.

Mid May-early June **KunstRAI**

www.kunstrai.nl
A hundred or so galleries, national and international, show work at this commercial five-day exhibition at RAI Convention Centre.

Mid May **National Windmill Day**

www.molens.nl/event/nationale-molendagen
On the second weekend in May, about 600 state-subsidised windmills open their doors and spin their sails, selling flour and bread made the traditional way.

Late May & Nov **Kunstvlaai**

www.kunstvlaai.nl
This biennial art market is the hipper twin to KunstRAI (*see above*), focusing on new artists and galleries at venues around the city.

Late May **Rollende Keukens**

www.rollendekeukens.nl
Street food festival 'Rolling Kitchens' is a much-loved event at Westergasfabriek, with bands and DJs providing a musical backdrop to the gastronomic weirdness.

Late May-early June **Open Ateliers: Kunstroute de Westelijke Eilanden**

www.oawe.nl
Artists living in the picturesque islands around Prinseneiland open their doors to the general public. The Jordaan hosts an Open Ateliers in late spring; details on www.openateliersjordaan.nl.

Late May-early June **Amsterdam Tattoo Convention**

www.tattooexpo.eu
The big names from the global tattoo scene swoop down on to the RAI Convention Centre to ink up everyone from bikers to housewives.

Summer

As spring merges into summer, both the calendar and the city become even more packed. Whether you want to party for 48 hours straight at a music festival, catch some rays from a canal boat or sit back and take it all in at Vondelpark, Amsterdam caters for every experience-seeker. However, if you're a first timer and don't want to spend half your holiday waiting in a lengthy museum queue, you may want to come back later in the year. Prices also tend to take a hike around this time – so if you're

Amsterdam Roots Festival

Angels & Demons, Sensation

On the third weekend in June, the owners of the beautiful, hidden gardens behind the city's posh canal houses open their doors, giving the public a chance to peek at these stunning secret gems.

Early July Pitch Festival
www.pitchfestival.nl
Pitch is an 'intelligent electro fest' at Westergasfabriek, geared towards left-field dance music.

Early July Amsterdam Roots Festival
www.amsterdamroots.nl
World music acts flock to play this four-day shindig at various venues across the city, culminating in a free open-air party in Oosterpark.

Early-mid July Over het IJ
www.overhetij.nl
This ten-day international festival at NDSM (*see p160*) celebrates adventurous theatre on a large scale, with a series of avant-garde theatrical projects.

Early July Sensation
www.sensation.com
This highlight of Amsterdam's dance music calendar at ArenA combines major house and techno DJs with mesmerising acrobatic dancers and pyrotechnic displays.

Early-mid July Julidans
www.julidans.nl
An international contemporary dance festival at various venues, featuring internationally renowned dance artists as well as newcomers.

Mid July-mid Aug Kwaku
www.kwakufestival.nl
'Kwaku' is the word that symbolises the emancipation of the people of Suriname and is also the name of this family festival, which takes place every weekend throughout the summer in the multicultural 'hood around ArenA stadium.

visiting between May and August, best book tickets in advance and eat at local haunts rather than tourist hotspots. But for a bona fide taste of Dutch life, complete with terrace parties, urban beaches and a Vitamin D-induced buzz, the city is at its finest in summer.

♥ June Holland Festival
www.hollandfestival.nl
This hugely popular month-long event (established in 1947) is the Netherlands' leading performing arts festival. It takes a refreshing approach to dance, literature, visual arts, theatre and film, but music is its central theme, particularly in the realms of contemporary classical, experimental and electronic music. It attracts international stars and composers each year, and you're guaranteed a series of groundbreaking premieres and reworkings that'll move on to make waves in other cultural capitals around the world. Book well in advance.

Late June Open Garden Days
www.opentuinendagen.nl

❤ Early Aug Amsterdam Gay Pride

www.amsterdamgaypride.nl
Although Gay Pride is always
surrounded by drama and
controversy to do with money,
politics and big egos, the
atmosphere during the boat parade
on the first Saturday in August
is simply fabulous and utterly
infectious. Over half a million
spectators line the Prinsengracht to
watch the boats, each with garish
decorations, a loud sound system
and a crew of bare-chested sailors.

Mid Aug De Parade

www.deparade.nl
Locals flock to eat, drink, be merry
and catch an act – cabaret, music,
comedy or drama – in Martin
Luther Kingpark.

Mid Aug Appelsap

www.appelsap.net
This outdoor hip hop festival in
Flevopark attracts around 15,000
visitors, and the programme
takes hip hop back to its roots and
includes up-and-coming artists as
well as local favourites.

❤ Mid Aug Grachtenfestival

www.grachtenfestival.nl
What started out in 1997 as a single
free concert from an orchestra
floating on a pontoon in front of
the Hotel Pulitzer has grown into
the 'Canal Festival'. Handel would
be delighted to hear that this
modern water music has expanded
to offer almost 100 classical music
concerts, set on or near the water.

Late Aug-early Sept Netherlands Theater Festival

www.tf.nl
This ten-day festival showcases
an edited selection of the best
Dutch and Belgian theatre of the
previous year. The accompanying
Fringe event brings a mix of more
experimental productions.

Amsterdam Gay Pride

Late Aug Uitmarkt

www.uitmarkt.nl
Over the last weekend in August,
the free Uitmarkt whets appetites
with previews of theatre, opera,
dance and music events.

Aug/Sept Magneet Festival

www.magneetfestival.nl
Magneet brings a bit of Burning
Man to a man-made stretch of
sand on Zeeburgereiland in Oost,
with a festival on four consecutive
weekends encompassing music,
theatre and experimental arts.

Autumn

The crowds of tourists fade away
in the autumn to reveal empty
cobbled streets covered in red,
yellow and gold leaves. Ironically,
it is now – as temperatures drop
and the nights draw in – that
Amsterdam's charm enters full
bloom. With picturesque canals
and cultural events galore, autumn
is the perfect time for a city break
before the chill sets in and street

wandering becomes limited. You'll find fewer visitors at the main tourist sights, so this is a great time for art lovers to spend hours at the city's showcase museums. Towards the end of the season, festive energy takes hold of the city, with various Christmas events and an appearance from the man himself, St Nicholas.

Early Sept City Swim
www.amsterdamcityswim.nl
The temperature is plummeting but that doesn't discourage 2,500 swimmers from jumping into the canals to swim a 2,000m (6,560ft) course to raise money for charity.

Mid Sept Open Monument Days
www.openmonumentendag.nl
Visit buildings that are normally closed to the public as part of European Heritage Days, involving around 4,000 sites across the Netherlands.

Late Sept Dam tot Damloop
www.damloop.nl
The Dam to Dam Run stretches 16.1km (10 miles) from Amsterdam to the town of Zaandam, and up to 250,000 people gather to watch almost 100,000 participants trying to finish within the two-hour limit.

Late Sept Unseen
www.unseenamsterdam.com
This 'photo fair with a festival flair' is based in Westergasfabriek but expands to other locations for exhibitions and lots of parties.

Mid Oct Cinekid
www.cinekid.nl
The five-day Cinekid is the largest child-oriented film festival on the planet, involving over 500 productions, from films to TV series to multimedia installations. Key venues are The Movies and Westergasfabriek.

❤ Mid Oct Amsterdam Dance Event
www.amsterdam-dance-event.nl
The organisers claim this five-day event is the world's largest festival of clubbing and dance music. It combines business with pleasure: during the day, there are conferences and workshops, while each night roughly 400 international acts and DJs will keep your feet moving with mind-blowing performances across the city. Amsterdam Music Festival (AMF) runs at the same time, showcasing the world's biggest DJs at the biggest venues in Amsterdam.

Mid Oct Amsterdamse Cello Biennale
www.cellobiennale.nl
Muziekgebouw (*see p162*) hosts this nine-day festival of concerts and masterclasses from musicians and ensembles from around the world.

Late Oct Amsterdam Spook Halloween Festival
www.halloweenamsterdam.com
An over-the-top party in a scary location is the main attraction, but the festival also includes plenty of other ghoul-infested activities.

Late Oct London Calling
www.londoncalling.nl
Taking place twice a year, this two-day indie music festival at Paradiso (*see p113*) is a showcase for new bands.

Late Oct PINT Bokbierfestival
www.pintbbf.nl
The Beurs van Berlage plays host to this three-day beer festival, the largest in the Netherlands. Check the website of PINT (a similar organisation to the UK's CAMRA).

Oct/Nov KLIK! Amsterdam Animation Festival
www.klikamsterdam.nl

For five fun-packed days, EYE Film Institute becomes the animation capital of Europe in a festival geared towards cartoon-lovers young and old.

Early Nov N8 (Museum Night)
www.n8.nl
On the first Saturday in November, most museums and galleries open late and organise something special to complement regular exhibits.

Late Nov International Documentary Filmfestival Amsterdam
www.idfa.nl
The biggest documentary festival in the world with Q&As, workshops and screenings throughout the city.

❤ Mid Nov-early Dec Sinterklaas
Sinterklaas (St Nicholas) kicks off three weeks of festivities by sailing down the Amstel into town on his steamboat. With a white beard, red robe and mitre, he parades around town on his horse, ending up at the Scheepvaartmuseum, while dozens of blacked-up Zwarte Pieten (Black Peters) hand out sweets. The celebrations continue, with little gifts being left in children's shoes at night, until Pakjesavond ('gift evening') on 5 December, when families exchange presents and poems.

Amsterdam Light Festival

Winter
Sure, it's cold (and most likely wet) outside but that doesn't dampen Amsterdam's warming display of seasonal cheer. From traditional Dickensian Christmas markets and ice skating to trendy festivals in converted industrial buildings, there's a winter attraction for just about everyone. What's more, Amsterdam has a host of cosy venues designed for eating, drinking and being merry, which come into their own as the cold sets in. Be wary of the festive price hikes, however; travelling during December can leave your wallet worse for wear. For many in the Netherlands, 5 December is the most important day of the festive season. Although 24 and 25 December are celebrated, the city doesn't grind to a halt, and many businesses stay open over Christmas.

Early Dec-mid Jan Amsterdam Light Festival
www.amsterdamlightfestival.com
Light sculptures and projections brighten up a route from the Amstel to the Maritime Museum.

31 Dec Oudejaarsavond (New Year's Eve)
A riot of champagne, *oliebollen* (deep-fried dough, apple and raisins) and fireworks on the streets near Nieuwmarkt and Dam Square.

Mid Jan FashionWeek
www.fashionweek.nl
Amsterdam FashonWeek puts the city on the fashion map, with catwalk shows in unique locations, plus exhibitions and readings.

Late Jan/early Feb Chinese New Year
Nieuwmarkt is a focal point for the annual festivities to mark Chinese New Year; expect lion dances, firecrackers, drums and gongs.

Amsterdam by Area

Bloemenmarkt

Getting Started

The heart of Amsterdam is the **Old Centre**, which is bounded by Prins Hendrikkade to the north, Oudeschans and Zwanenburgwal to the east, the Amstel to the south and Singel to the west. Within these borders, the Old Side, roughly covering the triangle formed by Centraal Station, the Nieuwmarkt and the Dam, is notorious for hosting the Red Light District (*see p76*). However, the area is also home to historical sights, including Oude Kerk (*see p75*) and De Waag.

The New Side, on the other hand, is the Old Side's gentler sister, featuring a history entwined with the intelligentsia, thanks to its many bookshops, brown cafés and the various buildings of the University of Amsterdam.

The **Grachtengordel** ('girdle of canals') that guards the Old Centre is idyllic and uniquely Dutch. It is also home to Anne Frank Huis (*see p100*) and the Westerkerk (*see p99*). The Western Canal Belt denotes the stretch of canals to the west and north of Leidsestraat, taking in Leidseplein, whereas Southern Canal Belt covers the area that lies to the east and Rembrandtplein.

The area around Waterlooplein, east of the Old Centre, was settled by Jews four centuries ago, hence its name, **Jodenbuurt**. This is in evidence at Joods Historisch Museum (*see p146*). Oases of flora occupy the **Plantage** neighbourhood, east and south-east of Waterlooplein, among them the Hortus Botanicus (*see p145*) and Artis (*see p144*).

Once the gateway to prosperity, Amsterdam's **Waterfront** has emerged as the setting for some of Europe's most inspired architecture. Traditional sights may be few, but the eastern stretch in particular has attracted thousands of new residents and developed into a boulevard of contemporary arts and nightlife. Across the IJ from Centraal, the redeveloped **Noord** is now one of the city's hippest areas – with its landmark A'DAM Toren (*see p153*) and futuristic EYE Film Institute (*see p154*).

Over in the other direction, the Westelijke Eilanden link up nicely with the charming **Jordaan**, bordered by Prinsengracht, Leidsegracht and Lijnbaansgracht. Working-class stalwarts here rub shoulders with affluent newcomers in an area steeped in character.

The **Museum Quarter** is a mix of culture – in the form of the Museumplein and its world-class Van Gogh Museum (*see p137*), Stedelijk Museum (*see p134*) and Rijksmuseum (*see p130*) – and couture, at the PC Hooftstraat. Nearby is the city's central green space, Vondelpark, separating the affluent and leafy **Oud West** neighbourhood and the business district, **Zuid**.

Against all the odds, **De Pijp** has remained a cultural melting pot, even though the area has been gentrified for several years. It proves that the city is still full of charm – you may not even feel the desire to enter a museum.

Getting around

Most sights lie within half an hour's walk from one another, and the excellent network of trams (see inside back cover for tram map) provides back-up for those low on energy. You can join the slipstream of locals on a bike or, better still, beg or borrow a boat to absorb the views on a cruise down the canals – surely the angle from which the city was meant to be seen. There's also a bewildering array of other modes of transport: metro, bus, ferry, and even horse and carriage (from Dam Square) or bike taxi (hail one near Dam Square, Damrak or Leidseplein).

Information and advice

The main tourist office, **Iamsterdam**, is outside Centraal Station, and there's another at Schiphol Airport. To start your research before arrival, head to www.Iamsterdam. com for all the key information you'll need.

Prices and discounts

Under 13s have free admission to many of the nation's museums. Even for older visitors, prices are still reasonable and rarely cost more than €17. However, if you're thinking of taking in a few museums in one go, then the **Museumkaart** (Museum Card or MK) is a steal at €59.90 for adults and €32.45 for under-19s (plus a €4.95 administration fee for first-timers). The card gives free or discounted admission to more than 400 attractions in the Netherlands, and is valid for one month. The museums with discounted or free entry for cardholders are denoted in this guide's listings by the letters 'MK'. Purchase the card at museums participating in the scheme.

The Amsterdam Tourist Board sells the **Iamsterdam City Card**, which gives you free entry to major museums, free rides on public transport and a complimentary canal trip, along with a 25 per cent discount at certain tourist attractions and restaurants. It costs €55 for 24 hours, €65 for 48 hours and €75 for 72 hours.

Tours

For first timers, guided tours are a great way to see the sights while hearing the stories from a local expert.

On foot
Self-guided walking tours are available for free download at www.Iamsterdam.com. If you'd rather soak up the knowledge of a local expert, try **Sanderman's New Amsterdam Free Walking Tour** (www.neweuropetours. eu/amsterdam). For foodies, **Eating Amsterdam Food Tours** (www.eatingamsterdamtours.com) are sure to satisfy.

On water
Canal bikes (pedalos) can be hired from major sights in the city for up to two hours of self-guided exploration. If you'd rather not navigate the crowded canals yourself, larger tourist boats, including **Amsterdam Canal Cruises** and **Canal Company**, pick up from the central Stadhouderskade.

💜 Cycle through the city

With over 800,000 in the city, there are almost more bikes than people in Amsterdam. What better way, then, to explore the 16th-century streets than on your own set of wheels? It's easy to see why the bike (or *fiets*) has been embraced as the city's preferred mode of transport, as cyclists are exceptionally well catered for, with flat roads and well-marked bike lanes.

When cycling, remember that unless indicated otherwise by signs, traffic from the right has priority, and watch out for pedestrians stepping into your path. Avoid catching your tyre in the tram rails (always cross at an angle) and never leave a bike unlocked – Amsterdam has one of the highest bicycle theft rates in the world.

With its prime location in the Old Centre, Dam Square is a great place to pick up a bike for your visit, but there are also dozens of rental shops throughout the city (*see p181* Getting Around). Keep in mind that if you're visiting during peak season or on a public holiday you'd do well to book in advance. Prices are €10-€20 per bike per day.

If you're unsteady and would rather cycle with a professional, there are plenty of guided bike tours on offer. Companies including **Yellow Bike** (620 6940, www.yellowbike.nl) and **Bike Tour Amsterdam** (5204 4351, www.biketouramsterdam.com) have starting points throughout the city. Free self-guided bike tours can also be downloaded from www.Iamsterdam.com.

Old Centre

The compelling Old Centre (aka Oud Centrum) surfs a wave of contradiction. On one side, the surface delights of shops jostle with the fine pursuits of the mind, whereas, on the other, the trappings of sex jar with the icons of religion. Marked off by Centraal Station, Singel and Zwanenburgwal, the area is bisected by Damrak, which turns into Rokin south of bustling Dam Square. The ancient Old Side (Oude Zijde) lies on the east, and the misleadingly titled New Side (Nieuwe Zijde) stretches to the west.

→ **Getting around**

Trams 1, 2, 4, 5, 9 13, 16, 17 and 26 run to and from Centraal Station, the transport hub of the city on the border of the Old Centre. For details of nearby canal cruises, see p98.

The Old Side

Once the most religious part of town, the Old Centre is now home to the notorious **Red Light District**. Despite its reputation, the area has seen something of a clean-up in recent years as city authorities have sought to restrict the number of prostitutes and coffeeshops in the hopes of attracting a classier line-up of shops, restaurants and tourists. While the sex industry is estimated to be worth around €500 million per year, most people just wander around, gazing at the live exhibits and taking in the history of the area at the **Erotic Museum** or **Hash Marihuana Hemp Museum**. At the centre of this illicit activity is **Oude Kerk** (Old Church), Amsterdam's oldest building, while the equally pious Museum **Ons' Lieve Heer op Solder** lies nearby.

At the bottom of Zeedijk, the castle-like **De Waag** (Weigh House) stands in the centre of Nieuwmarkt. Dating from 1488, it was built as a gatehouse and later contained an anatomical theatre. Yet more relative tranquility exists on the Nes, home to many of the city's theatres and several charming cafés. Nearby is the Oudemanhuis Book Market. People have traded books, prints and sheet music here since the 18th century.

Sights & museums

Allard Pierson Museum

Oude Turfmarkt 127 (525 2556, www.allardpiersonmuseum. nl). Tram 4, 9, 14, 16, 24. **Open** *10am-4.30pm Tue-Fri; 1-5pm Sat, Sun.* **Admission** *€10; €5 reductions; free under-4s, Iamsterdam, MK.* **Map** *p72 K10.*

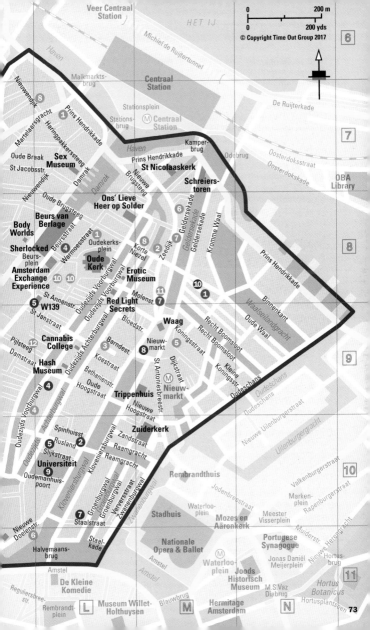

Best museum
Explore the city's DNA at the Amsterdam Museum (*p88*).

Unique shopping
Pre-loved bargains at Bij Ons Vintage (*p94*) and high design (and price tags) at Hôtel Droog (*p84*).

Cultural fix
Frascati (*p85*) – the home of progressive Dutch theatre. Puppets with a difference at Amsterdam Marionetten Theater (*p85*).

Meals to share
Café Bern for a cheese feast (*p80*) and cheap but terrific Chinese food at Nam Kee (*p81*).

Drinks with a difference
Refined cocktails with a view at MR PORTER (*p93*) or *jenever* at the historic Wynand Fockink (*p83*).

Big night out
Cool alternative music venue Bitterzoet (*p94*) or mainstream party palace Disco Dolly (*p94*).

Escape the buzz
Pay an early morning visit to Begijnhof's courtyard (*p90*) and Ons' Lieve Heer op Solder's (*p79*) 17th-century attic church.

Must-see sights
Stroll the Red Light District (*p76*) to see Amsterdam's oldest trade and visit 800-year-old Oude Kerk (*p75*) in the heart of sin city.

Established in 1934, the Allard Pierson is the University of Amsterdam's archaeological museum. It's home to one of the world's richest university collections, and contains archaeological exhibits from Ancient Egypt, Greece, Rome and the Near East. Admission includes entrance to **Bijzondere Collecties** (*see below*).

Bijzondere Collecties

Oude Turfmarkt 129 (525 7300, www.bijzonderecollecties.uva.nl). Tram 4, 9, 14, 16, 24. **Reading room** *9.30am-5pm Mon-Fri.* **Exhibition** *10am-5pm Tue-Fri; 1-5 Sat, Sun.* **Admission** *€7.50; €3.75-€6.50 reductions; concession discounts available; free Iamsterdam, MK.* **Map** *p72 K11.*
They like their paper products at the University of Amsterdam's 'Special Collections': documents, prints, maps, photos and endless rows of books. The invaluable pre-1850 collection is especially

strong on the history of printing, Hebrew and Judaica studies, Protestantism and medicine; the post-1850 collection focuses more on meritorious design, with exhibitions ranging from Shakespeare in the Netherlands to sacred books from Ethiopia. The shop has an excellent selection of design-related books. Admission includes entrance to the **Allard Pierson Museum** (*see p72*).

Erotic Museum

Oudezijds Achterburgwal 54 (627 8954, www.erotisch-museum.nl). Tram 4, 9, 14, 16, 24 or Metro Nieuwmarkt. **Open** *11am-1am Sun-Thur, 11am-2pm Fri, Sat.* **Admission** *€7. No cards.* **Map** *p72 L8.*
The **Sexmuseum** (Damrak 18, www.sexmuseumamsterdam.nl) may benefit from its Damrak site in terms of passing trade, but the Erotic Museum is in the more appropriate location: slap bang in the middle of the Red Light District.

Hash Marihuana & Hemp Museum

That's not to say, though, that it's any more authentic or interesting. Its prize exhibits are a bicycle-powered dildo and a few of John Lennon's erotic drawings, while lovers of Bettie Page (and there are many) will enjoy the original photos of the S&M muse on display. It also puts on temporary exhibits in the Sexy Art Gallery on the third floor. In general, the museum's name is somewhat inaccurate: despite its best intentions and desperate desire to shock, it's as unsexy as can be. You're probably best off going to one of the many nearby sex shops for your kicks.

Hash Marihuana & Hemp Museum
Oudezijds Achterburgwal 148 (624 8926, www.hashmuseum. com). Tram 4, 9, 14, 16, 24 or Metro Nieuwmarkt. **Open** *10am-10pm daily.* **Admission** *€9; free under-13s (must be accompanied by an adult).* **Map** *p72 L9.*
Cannabis connoisseurs will lose themselves ogling larger-than-

life pictures of perfect plants and gleaming balls of hash in this museum in the Red Light District. But this shrine to skunk is not only for smokers. Strait-laced visitors will be entertained by the detailed history of the plant. There's plenty of pro-cannabis propaganda too, including information about its medicinal uses, the environmental benefits of hemp and the cannabis culture of today. Don't miss the indoor 'grow-op' that showcases plants being lovingly cultivated for their seeds, guarded by a guru of ganja, who offers advice.

♥ Oude Kerk
Oudekerksplein 23 (625 8284, www.oudekerk.nl). Tram 4, 9, 16, 24 or Metro Nieuwmarkt. **Open** *10am-6pm Mon-Sat; 1-5.30pm Sun.* **Admission** *€10, €7.50 reductions; free under-13s, Iamsterdam, MK. No cards.* **Map** *p72 L8*
Built in 1306 as a wooden chapel, and renovated and extended between 1330 and 1571, the Oude Kerk is the city's oldest and most

💜 Walk through the Red Light District

Begin at the entrance to Zeedijk, where the district's debauchery began in the 15th and 16th centuries. The **Prins Hendrik Hotel** at Prins Hendrikkade 53 (623 7969, prins-hendrik. hotelamsterdam.net) is where jazz legend Chet Baker took his final curtain call in 1988 – on to a cement parking pole – from a window (second floor on the left). You'll see a brass plaque commemorating the crooning trumpeter has been put up to the left of the hotel's entrance. Continuing along Zeedijk, you'll find **Casablanca** (no.26), one of the few after-hours spots still functioning as a shadow of what it was. Before his death, Chet came to jam and hang out at this club alongside fellow crooner Gerry Mulligan in the 1950s. Further down at no.63 is **Café 't Mandje** (see p81), where the first openly gay establishment appeared in the 1930s, closed and then reopened. Back then, the subculture marked Zeedijk as a place where heroin could be scored with comparative ease and Amsterdam's reputation subsequently became littered with needles and foil. There was even a time when a German tour operator tried to run a 'criminal safari' along Zeedijk and street cleaners needed armed escorts, but as you'll notice nowadays the street is very safe.

At the next intersection, either continue south on Zeedijk into the heart of Amsterdam's tiny **Chinatown** (see p81) or make a right on Korte Niezel and turn left before you cross the bridge to land in the district's main drag, **Oudezijds Achterburgwal**,

which is dominated by smut. A short walk away at no.37 is the **Bananenbar** (627 8954, www. bananenbar.nl), where improbably dexterous female genitalia can be seen performing night after night – and, as the central part of their belief-beggaring act, spitting out an average 15kg (33lb) of fruit every evening. A former owner of the Bananenbar once tried to stave off taxmen – and get round the fact that his drinking licence had lapsed – by picking Satan as a deity and registering the Bananenbar as a church. It was a scam that worked for years – until 1988, when the 'Church of Satan' claimed a membership of 40,000 overseen by a council of nine anonymous persons. The tax police were called in to bust the joint, but the bar was tipped off and the 'church' disbanded. Now under the same ownership as the

Erotic Museum (*see p74*), the Bananenbar has kept its name and returned to its roots as a purveyor of sleaze. When you reach the next bridge, make a right on **Molensteeg** to cross the canal before continuing left down Oudezijds Achterburgwal on the opposite side. Stop in at no.60, the **Red Light Secrets Museum of Prostitution** (*see p78*), which although tourist-orientated, does allow you a glimpse behind the scenes, enabling visitors to empathise with the job of the sex worker. Further down at no.106 you'll find **Casa Rosso** nightclub (627 8954, www.casarosso.nl). This is one of Amsterdam's most popular venues for live erotic entertainment, should you be wishing to tick that off your bucket list.

If you want to see Red Light ladies in all their window-working glory, take your next right down **Stoofsteeg** – just make sure your camera is well away. Featuring an eclectic mix of window workers and cafés, the narrow passageway is apt reflection of the controversial gentrification transforming the area.

Make a right on **Oudezijds Voorburgwal** and ogle the array of sex shops and erotic boutiques on your way back to **Oude Kerk** (*see p75*), Amsterdam's oldest building and church, ironically situated in the centre of its sin city. See if you can spot the small brass bosom laid by a mystery artist into the pavement by the front entrance. For more on the sex work industry, finish up at the **Prostitution Information Centre** (Enge Kerk Steeg 3, 420 7328, www.pic-amsterdam.com).

Oude Kerk

interesting church. One can only imagine the Sunday Mass chaos during its heyday of the mid 1500s, when it contained 38 altars, each with its own guild-sponsored priest. The original furnishings were removed during the Reformation, but the church has retained its wooden roof, which was painted in the 15th century with figurative images. Look out for the Gothic and Renaissance façade above the northern portal, and the stained-glass windows, which date from the 16th and 17th centuries. Rembrandt's wife, Saskia, who died in 1642, is buried here.

The inscription over the bridal chamber, which translates as 'Marry in haste, mourn at leisure,' is in keeping with the church's location in the heart of the Red Light District, though this is more by accident than design. If you want to be semi-shocked, check out the carvings in the choir benches of men evacuating their bowels – apparently they tell a moralistic tale. Now the church is as much an exhibition centre as anything else.

Red Light Secrets Museum of Prostitution

Oudezijds Achterburgwal 60H (846 7020, www.redlightsecrets. com) Tram 4, 9, 14, 16, 24 or Metro Nieuwmarkt. **Open** *11am-midnight daily.* **Admission** *€8.* **Map** *p72 L8.*
Set inside a 17th-century canal house, Red Light Secrets allows

♥ Ons' Lieve Heer op Solder

Oudezijds Voorburgwal 38 (624 6604, www.opsolder.nl). Tram 4, 9, 16, 24 or Metro Nieuwmarkt. **Open** *10am-5pm Mon-Sat; 1-5pm Sun.* **Admission** *€10; €5 reductions; free under-5s, Iamsterdam, MK.* **Map** *p72 L8.*

'Our Lord in the Attic' is one of Amsterdam's most unusual spots and used to be one of its best-kept secrets. Visitors can explore the narrow corridors of the lower canal house, which have been wonderfully preserved since the 17th century, and imagine what life might have been like in the Dutch Golden Age. It's fascinating to walk through the historically furnished living rooms, kitchens and bedrooms, but the main attraction is clear when you arrive upstairs to find a church in the attic.

Built in 1663, this attic church was used by Catholics when they were banned from public worship after the Alteration. The authorities knew of the then-illicit activity but turned a blind eye. Their actions (or lack thereof) were an appropriate reflection of the religious tolerance in the Netherlands, which is a central theme at the museum today. The attic has been beautifully preserved, and the altarpiece features a painting by the 18th-century artist Jacob de Wit. It's the second oldest museum in the city, after the Rijkmuseum, and in 2015 was extended into the neighbouring building at Oudezijds Voorburwal 38. It's open for at least four hours every day and is still often used for services.

visitors to step into the intriguing world of Amsterdam's oldest trade. Although it's very much on the tourist trail, Red Light Secrets provides information about the history of the profession along with secrets and stories from the women themselves. Guests can even experience sitting inside a shop window, and it might be the only one in the district which allows you to take photos.

Restaurants & cafés

De Bakkerswinkel €

Warmoesstraat 69 (489 8000, www.debakkerswinkel.nl). Tram 1, 2, 4, 5, 9, 13, 16, 17, 24. **Open** *8am-5.30pm Mon-Fri; 9am-6pm Sat, Sun.* **Map** *p72 L8* ❶ *Café*
A bakery-tearoom where you can indulge in lovingly prepared and hearty sandwiches, soups and the most divine slabs of quiche.

Bird €€

Zeedijk 72-74 & 77 (620 1442 restaurant, 420 6289 snack bar, www.thai-bird.nl). Tram 4, 9, 16, 24 or Metro Nieuwmarkt. **Restaurant** *noon-11pm daily.* **Snack bar** *1-10pm Mon-Wed; 1-10.30pm Thur-Sun.* **Map** *p72 M8* ❷ *Thai*
The most authentic Thai place in town. As a result, it's also the most crowded, but the food is worth the wait. The snack bar is at no.77; the restaurant is across the street at nos.72-74 and is the best choice if you plan to linger.

Blauw aan de Wal €€€

Oudezijds Achterburgwal 99 (330 2257, www.blauwaandewal. com). Tram 4, 9, 16, 24 or Metro Nieuwmarkt. **Open** *6-11.30pm Mon-Sat.* **Map** *p72 L9* ❸ *Mediterranean*
The hallmarks of this mainstay in the heart of the Red Light District, complete with a

peaceful courtyard, are tempting Mediterranean dishes and a wine list to inspire visiting oenophiles.

Bridges €€€€

Oudezijds Voorburgwal 197 (555 3560, www.bridgesrestaurant.nl). Tram 4, 9, 14, 16, 24. **Open** *noon-2.30pm, 6.30-10.30pm Tue-Fri; 1-3pm, 6.30-10.30pm Sat, Sun.* **Map** *p72 K9* ❹ *Fish & seafood*
The Bridges restaurant in The Grand Amsterdam hotel (*see p174*) is a committed proponent of slow food. The menu features locally caught, seasonal seafood and five-star ingredients, such as oysters and caviar. Be sure to admire the Karel Appel mural upon entering.

❤ Café Bern €€

Nieuwmarkt 9 (622 0034, www. cafebern.com). Tram 4, 9, 14, 16, 24 or Metro Nieuwmarkt. **Open** *4pm-1am (kitchen 6-11pm) daily.* **No cards.** **Map** *p72 M9* ❺ *Swiss*
Despite its Swiss origins, the Dutch adopted the cheese fondue as a national dish long ago. Sample its culinary conviviality at this cosy 'brown café', which was established by a nuclear physicist who knew his way round the fusion of cheese with wine. Book ahead.

Dum Dum Palace €€

Zeedijk 37 (304 4966, www. dumdum.nl). Tram 4, 9, 14, 16, 24 or Metro Nieuwmarkt. **Open** *11am-1am Sun-Thur; 11am-3am Fri, Sat.* **Map** *p72 M8* ❻ *Restaurant/bar*
One of the new(er) players in Chinatown, this brasserie has been wowing visitors since it secretly opened its doors in 2016. Buzzing Asian restaurant by day, the wooden-decorated venue transforms into a bar by night. Crowd favourites include beef stew over fries, and teriyaki chicken.

Juice by Nature €
Warmoesstraat 108 (www. juicebynature.com). Tram 1, 2, 4, 5, 9, 13, 14, 16, 17, 24. **Open** *9am-8pm Mon-Fri; 10am-8pm Sat, Sun.* **Map** *p72 L8* ❿ *Juice bar/café*
Providing a contrast to the grunge bars in De Wallen, Juice by Nature has set out to 'make healthy delicious', with a mouth-watering offering of cold-pressed juices, coffee, salads and sandwiches.

♥ Nam Kee €€
Zeedijk 111-113 (624 3470, www. namkee.net). Tram 4, 9, 14, 16, 24 or Metro Nieuwmarkt. **Open** *noon-11pm daily.* **No cards.** **Map** *p72 M8* ⓫ *Chinese*
Cheap and terrific food has earned this Chinese joint a devoted following: the oysters in black bean sauce has achieved classic status. If it's too crowded, try one of the equally excellent nearby alternatives: **New King** (Zeedijk 115-117, 625 2180), **Wing Kee** (Zeedijk 76, 623 5683) or **Si Chuan** (Warmoesstraat 17, 420 7833).

Bars
Bierfabriek
Nes 67 (528 9910, www.bierfabriek. com). Tram 4, 9, 14, 16, 24. **Open** *3pm-1am Mon-Thur; 3pm-2am Fri; 1pm-2am Sat; 1pm-1am Sun.* **Map** *p72 K10* ❷
With an industrial look and laid-back attitude, the 'Beer Factory' pulls in a young crowd for its own-brewed beers and excellent roast chicken.

Bubbles & Wines
Nes 37 (422 3318, www. bubblesandwines.com). Tram 4, 9, 14, 16, 24. **Open** *3.30pm-1am Mon-Sat; 2-9pm Sun.* **Map** *p72 K9* ❸
This long, low-ceilinged room has the feel of a wine cellar, albeit one with mood lighting and banquettes. There are more than 50

wines available by the glass and 180 by the bottle, with accompanying posh nosh (including Osetra caviar, truffle cheese and foie gras).

Café de Jaren
Nieuwe Doelenstraat 20-22 (625 5771, www.cafedejaren.nl). Tram 4, 9, 14, 16, 24. **Open** *8.30am-1am Mon-Thur; 8.30am-2am Fri, Sat; 8.30am-1am Sun.* **Map** *p72 K11* ❻
All of Amsterdam – students, tourists, lesbigays, cinemagoers, the fashion pack – comes to this former bank for lunch, coffee or something stronger, all day long, making it sometimes difficult to bag a seat. Upstairs becomes a restaurant after 5.30pm. Be prepared to fight for a spot on the Amstel-side terrace in summer.

Café 't Mandje
Zeedijk 63 (622 5375, www. cafetmandje.amsterdam). Tram 4, 9, 16, 24 or Metro Nieuwmarkt. **Open** *5pm-1am Tue-Thur; 4pm-3am Fri; 3pm-3am Sat; 3pm-1am Sun.* **No cards.** **Map** *p72 M8* ❼
Launched more than 80 years ago, this historic café was the city's first (moderately) openly gay and lesbian bar. The original proprietor, Bet van Beeren (who died over 40 years ago), was legendary for her

In the know
Tiny Chinatown

A string of no-frills restaurants, food shops and a Buddhist temple on the Zeedijk, winding from Centraal Station towards Nieuwmarkt, makes up what is perhaps the world's smallest Chinatown. Here, you can eat authentic fare for a tenner or pick up the ingredients to cook an Asian feast at home. The area is where to experience street celebrations for Chinese New Year, including a traditional lion dance performed with live drumming.

TonTon Club

role as (probably) the world's first lesbian biker chick. After years of closure, the café reopened in 2012 to suggest that time can stand still.

Mata Hari

Oudezijds Achterburgwal 22 (205 0919, www.matahari-amsterdam. nl). Tram 1, 2, 4, 5, 9, 13, 16, 17, 24 or Metro Nieuwmarkt. **Open** *noon-1am Mon-Thur; noon-3am Fri, Sat; noon-1am Sun.* **Map** *p72 M8* 8
Named after the exotic but tricksy Dutch courtesan, it's appropriate that this bar and lounge has brought a touch of comfort and class to the Red Light District. Sympathetic lighting, retro furniture and an open kitchen serving dishes such as 'chocolate salami with forget-me-not liqueur' make the seduction complete.

TonTon Club Centrum

Sint Annendwarsstraat 6 (www. tontonclub.nl). Tram 4, 9, 16, 24 or Metro Nieuwmarkt. **Open** *4pm-midnight Mon, Tue; noon-midnight Wed-Sun.* **No cards.** **Map** *p72 L8* 10
This arcade bar in the heart of the Red Light District does feature old-school games such as pinball, but most have been hacked to do such things as print out chocolate – making TonTon more of a meeting place for local game designers and artists. Besides offering coffee, beer and snacks, TonTon also regularly brings in chefs to provide meals – from Korean tacos to Dutch weed burgers.

Van Kerkwijk

Nes 41 (620 3316, www. caferestaurant vankerkwijk. nl). Tram 4, 9, 14, 16, 24. **Open** *11am-1am daily.* **Map** *p72 K9* 11
Far from the bustle of Dam Square, though really just a few strides away on one of Amsterdam's most charming streets, Van Kerkwijk is airy by day, romantic and candlelit by night. You'll find sandwiches at lunch and more substantial food in the evening, though the emphasis is as much on genteel drinking. Beware the near-vertical stairs down to the toilets.

tables, it's all about the weed here – but the coffee is also outstanding.

Greenhouse Centrum
Oudezijds Voorburgwal 191 (www. greenhouse.org). Tram 4, 9, 14, 16, 24. Open 9am-1am daily. No cards. Map p72 L9 ❹
This legendary coffeeshop offers potent weed with some strong prices to match – it's won the High Times Cannabis Cup more than 30 times. The Grand Hotel is next door, so the occasional celebrity stops by to get hammered. The vibe inside has grown quite commercial, but it's still worth a peek, if only to see the beautiful interior with its sunken floors, mosaic stones and blown-glass lamps.

Rusland
Rusland 16 (845 6434, www. coffeeshop-rusland-amsterdam. com). Tram 4, 9, 14, 16, 24 or Metro Nieuwmarkt. Open 8am-12.30am daily. No cards. Map p72 L10 ❺
Well known as the longest-running coffeeshop in the city, this 'Russian' den has hardwood floors and colourful cushions that complement an efficient multi-level design. The top-floor bar serves more than 40 different loose teas and healthy fruit shakes, while below there's a decent pipe display.

❤ Wynand Fockink
Pijlsteeg 31 (639 2695, www. wynand-fockink.nl). Tram 4, 9, 14, 16, 24. Open 3-9pm daily. No cards. Map p72 K9 ⑫
It's standing room only at this historic tasting house. Hidden behind the Grand Hotel Krasnapolsky, and unchanged since 1679, this has been a meeting place for Freemasons since the beginning; past visitors include Churchill and Chagall. The menu of liqueurs and *jenevers* reads like a list of unwritten novels: Parrot Soup; The Longer the Better; Rose Without Thorns.

Coffeeshops
Basjoe
Kloveniersburgwal 62 (no phone or website). Metro Nieuwmarkt. Open 10am-1am daily. No cards. Map p72 L10 ❷
The canal view alone places Basjoe among our favourite coffeeshops in Amsterdam. Candlelit, with a plain decor of terracotta soft vinyl booths, cream walls and wooden

---

Shops & services
Condomerie
Warmoesstraat 141 (627 4174, www.condomerie.com). Tram 4, 9, 14, 16, 24 or Metro Nieuwmarkt. Open 11am-9pm Mon, Wed-Sat; 11am-6pm Tue; 1-6pm Sun. Map p72 L9 ❺ *Sex shop*
A variety of rubbers of the non-erasing kind, to wrap up trouser snakes of all shapes and sizes, in a store that's equal parts amusing and inspiring.

Hôtel Droog

💜 Hôtel Droog
Staalstraat 7 (523 5059, www. droog.com). Tram 4, 9, 14, 16, 24. **Open** *9am-7pm daily.* **Map** *p72 L10* ❼ *Homewares*
Dutch design dynamo Droog expanded its HQ into a flagship 'hotel' – a city-centre design mall where you can attend a lecture or an exhibition, get beauty advice at Cosmania and, yes, even spend the night in the single suite. The historic building's rag trade origins continue at ice-cool boutique Kabinet. The Droog shop still sells some of the wittiest ranges around: Jurgen Bey, Richard Hutten, Hella Jongerius and Marcel Wanders.

Nieuwmarkt Antique Market
Nieuwmarkt (no phone or website). Tram 4, 9, 14, 16, 24 or Metro Nieuwmarkt. **Open** *May-Oct 9am-5pm Sun.* **Map** *p72 M9* ❽ *Market*
A few streets away from the ladies in the windows, this antiques and bric-a-brac market attracts browsers looking for other kinds of pleasures: old books, furniture and objets d'art.

Oudemanhuis Book Market
Oudemanhuispoort (no phone or website). Tram 4, 9, 14, 16, 24. **Open** *9am-5pm Mon-Sat.* **No cards.** **Map** *p72 L10* ❾ *Market*
People have been buying and selling books, prints and sheet music from this indoor row of shops since the 18th century.

De Wijnerij
Binnen Bantammerstraat 8 (625 6433, www.dewijnerij.com). Tram 4, 9, 14, 16, 24 or Metro Nieuwmarkt. **Open** *11am-6.30pm Tue-Fri; 10am-6.30pm Sat.* **Map** *p72 M8* ❿ *Drink*
This friendly and passionate shop specialises in French wine – usually from organic producers – and unique local distillates such as *jenever*. With another wine and liquor shop, **De Twee Engelen** (no.19), and the relaxed café/terrace **Café Captein en Co** (no.27), this street is a delight for thirsty people.

Entertainment

♥ Amsterdam Marionetten Theater

Nieuwe Jonkerstraat 8 (620 8027, www.marionettentheater.nl). Tram 4, 9 or Metro Nieuwmarkt. **Box office** *online until 2hrs before the performance, last minute only by telephone. Tickets €7.50-€15.* **Map** *p72 M8* ❶ *Theatre*

Imagine hand-crafted wooden marionettes wearing silk and velvet costumes, wielded by puppeteers in classic works by Mozart and Offenbach, and you'll have an idea of what the AMT is all about. One of the last outposts of an old European tradition, the theatre also offers lunches, dinners or high teas, to be taken while the puppets perform.

Eagle Amsterdam

Warmoesstraat 90 (808 5283, www.theeagleamsterdam.com). Tram 4, 9, 6. **Open** *11pm-4am Mon-Thur, Sun; 11pm-5am Fri, Sat.* **Map** *p72 L8* ❹ *Gay club*

Popular men-only cruise bar with 35 years of history. Eagle has a reputation for sexy and friendly punters, but dirty toilets and unfriendly staff – and can get absolutely packed. The downstairs darkroom is always action-filled, with cosy benches should you want to get intimate.

♥ Frascati

Nes 63 (626 6866, www.frascatitheater.nl). Tram 4, 9, 16. **Box office** *5.30-7.30pm Tue-Sat, or online. Tickets prices vary.* **Map** *p72 K10* ❺ *Theatre*

Frascati has been a cornerstone of progressive Dutch theatre since the 1960s and gives promising artists the chance to showcase their productions on one of its three stages. Its mission is to team up professionally trained artists with those from the street, resulting in a variety of theatre and dance shows.

Winston Kingdom

Warmoesstraat 131 (623 1380, www.winston.nl). Tram 1, 2, 4, 5, 9, 13, 14, 16, 17, 24. **Open** *9pm-4am Mon, Wed, Thur, Sun; 10pm-4am Tue; 9pm-5am Fri, Sat.* **Admission** *€5-€15.* **No cards.** **Map** *p72 M8* ❼ *Club*

An intimate venue downstairs from the Winston Hotel (*see p177*) that attracts a mixed crowd with its alternative rock and indie-tronica. Bands, from garage and folk to funky hip hop and ska, perform daily, followed by alternative DJs.

The New Side

Straight up from Centraal Station, just beyond touristy Damrak and the Beurs van Berlage, lies **Dam Square**, the heart of the city since the first dam was built across the Amstel here in 1270. Once a hub of social and political activities, today it's a convenient meeting point for tourists, the majority of whom convene under the **National Monument**, a 22-metre (70-foot) white obelisk dedicated to the Dutch servicemen who died in World War II. The west side of the square is flanked by the **Koninklijk Paleis** (Royal Palace) and the 600-year-old **Nieuwe Kerk**.

In the know
Caught short

Public toilets are few and far between in the city, though the four-bowls-in-one, grey plastic 'Rocket' urinals and high-tech 'Uri-liften' – which rise out of the ground – were permanently installed in the city's main nightlife squares. Apart from nipping into a café or department store, there are fewer choices for females. Install the Toilocator app before hitting the town or check out www.hogenood.nu to locate the nearest conveniences.

The **Spui** is the square that caps the area's three main arteries, which start down near the west end of Centraal Station: shopping street Kalverstraat, Nieuwezijds Voorburgwal and the Spuistraat.

The nearby **Begijnhof** is a group of houses built around a secluded courtyard and garden. Established in the 14th century, it provided modest homes for the Beguines, a religious sisterhood. Nowadays it's the best known of the city's many *hofjes* (almshouses). Next door is the excellent **Amsterdam Museum**, which tells the history of the city through imaginative displays.

The Spui plays host to many markets – the most notable being the **book market** on Fridays. Look out for the 'Lieverdje' (Little Darling) statue in front of the Athenaeum Nieuwscentrum store, a small, spindly and guano-smeared statue of a boy in goofy knee socks.

Leave Spui by going up Kalverstraat to the **Munttoren** (Mint Tower) at Muntplein. Right across from the Bloemenmarkt floating flower market, this medieval tower was once the western corner of Regulierspoort, a gate in the city wall in the late 15th century. The Munttoren is prettiest when it's floodlit at night, but daytime visitors may enjoy hearing its carillon ringing out at noon.

Koninklijk Paleis

Sights & museums

Body Worlds: The Happiness Project

Damrak 66 (0900 8411 €0.45/min, www.bodyworlds.nl). Tram 4, 9, 16, 24. **Open** *9am-8pm Mon-Fri, Sun; 9am-10pm Sat.* **Admission** *€18; €16 reductions; free under-6s.* **Map** *p72 K8.*

People seem to love donating their bodies to be plastinated for posterity. German anatomist Dr Gunther von Hagens now has 13,000 such corpses touring the world; since 2014, 200 of these have been on display in Amsterdam, to illustrate the relationship between anatomy and happiness.

Koninklijk Paleis

Dam (522 6161, info@dkh.nl for tours, www.paleisamsterdam. nl). Tram 1, 2, 4, 5, 9, 13, 14, 16, 17, 24. **Open** *10am-5pm Tue-Sun.* **Admission** *€10; €9 reductions; free under-18s, MK.* **Map** *p72 J9.*

Designed along classical lines by Jacob van Campen in the 17th century and built on 13,659 wooden piles that were rammed deep into the sand, the Royal Palace was originally built and used as Amsterdam's city hall. The poet Constantijn Huygens hyped it as 'the world's Eighth Wonder', a monument to the cockiness Amsterdam felt at the dawn of its Golden Age. The city hall was intended as a smugly epic 'screw

❤ Amsterdam Museum

Kalverstraat 92 (523 1822, www. amsterdammuseum.nl). Tram 1, 2, 4, 5, 9, 14, 16, 24. **Open** *10am-5pm daily.* **Admission** *€12.50; €6.50-€10 reductions; free under-4s, Iamsterdam, MK.* **Map** *p72 J10.*

A note to all those historical museums around the world that struggle to present their exhibits in an engaging fashion: head here to see how it's done. Amsterdam's historical museum is a gem – illuminating, interesting and entertaining.

It starts with the very buildings in which it's housed: a lovely, labyrinthine collection of 17th-century constructions built on the site of a 1414 nunnery, complete with its own brewery and livestock. The property was turned into an orphanage in 1578, which hundreds of children called home for almost four centuries until 1960. The Amsterdam Museum moved to the location in 1975, having started in the Waag as a branch of the City Museum. You can enter where it all began down Sint Luciensteeg, just off Kalverstraat, or off Spui, walking past the **Begijnhof** (*see p90*) and then through the grand **Civic Guard Gallery**, a small covered street hung with huge 16th- and 17th-century group portraits of wealthy burghers, as well as more modern works.

It continues with a computer-generated map of the area showing how Amsterdam has grown (and shrunk) throughout the last 800 years or so. It then takes a chronological trip through Amsterdam's past, using archaeological finds, works

of art and some far quirkier displays to show the city's rise from fishing village to ecstasy capital. One of its most popular recent exhibitions was 100 Years of Schiphol, paying tribute to the progression from muddy pasture to one of Europe's largest high-tech airports, and Amsterdam DNA – the museum's permanent exhibit which gives an hour-long highly engaging overview of Amsterdam's history, based on the city's core values of entrepreneurship, free thinking, citizenship and creativity.

you' gesture to visiting monarchs, a subspecies of humanity the people of Amsterdam had thus far happily done without. It was transformed into a royal palace during harder times, after Napoleon had made his brother, Louis, King of the Netherlands in 1808; this era can be traced through the fine collection of furniture on display inside.

The exterior is only really impressive when viewed from the rear, where Atlas holds his 1,000kg (2,200lb) copper load at a great height. It's even grander inside than out: the Citizens' Hall, with its baroque decoration in marble and bronze that depicts a miniature universe (with Amsterdam at its centre), is meant to make you feel about as worthy as the rats seen carved in stone over the Bankruptcy Chamber's door. The Palace became state property in 1936 but the Dutch royal family still use it to impress international guests.

Nieuwe Kerk

Dam Square (638 6909, www. nieuwekerk.nl). Tram 1, 2, 4, 5, 9, 13, 14, 16, 17, 24. **Open** *10am-5pm daily, but hrs may vary.* **Admission** *€16; €4.50-€14.40 reductions; free under-11s. Temporary exhibitions vary. No cards.* **Map** *p72 K8.*

While the 'old' Oude Kerk in the Red Light District was built in the 1300s, the sprightly 'new' Nieuwe Kerk dates from 1408. It's not known how much damage was caused by the fires of 1421 and 1452, or even how much rebuilding took place, but most of the pillars and walls were erected after that time. Iconoclasm in 1566 left the church intact, though statue and altars were removed in the Reformation. The sundial on its tower was used to set the time on all the city's clocks until 1890. In 1645, Nieuwe Kerk was gutted by the Great Fire; the ornate oak pulpit and great organ (the latter designed by Jacob van Campen) are thought to have been constructed after the blaze.

Also of interest here is the tomb of naval hero Admiral de Ruyter (1607-76), who initiated the ending of the Second Anglo-Dutch war – wounding British pride in the process – when he sailed up the Medway in 1667, inspiring a witness, Sir William Batten, to observe: 'I think the Devil shits Dutchmen.' Poets and Amsterdam natives PC Hooft and Joost van den Vondel are also buried here. These days, the Nieuwe Kerk hosts organ recitals, state occasions and consistently excellent exhibitions, including World Press Photo.

Restaurants & cafés

Gartine €

Taksteeg 7 (320 4132, www.gartine. nl). Tram 4, 9, 14, 16, 24. **Open** *10am-6pm Wed-Sun.* **No cards.** **Map** *p72 J10* ❼ *Tearoom*
Open only for breakfast, lunch and a full-blown high tea, Gartine is a testament to slow food, served by a friendly couple who grow their own veg and herbs in a greenhouse. Simple but marvellous.

Gebroeders Niemeijer €

Nieuwendijk 35 (707 6752, www. gebroedersniemeijer.nl). Tram 1, 2, 5, 13, 17. **Open** *8.15am-5.30pm Tue-Fri; 8.30am-5pm Sat; 9am-5pm Sun.* **Map** *p72 L7* ❽
Bakery/café
In stark contrast to the rest of the dingy street it's on, Gebroeders Niemeijer is an artisanal French bakery and bright, light tearoom that serves breakfast and lunch. All the breads and pastries are made by hand and baked in a stone oven. Sausages come from local producers Brandt en Levie and cheeses from the city's best French cheese purveyor, **Kef** (Marnixstraat 192, www.kaasvankef.nl). Perfect.

❤ Begijnhof

*Begijnhof 30 (622 19 18, www.
nicolaas-parochie.nl). Tram 1, 2,
4, 5, 9, 14, 16, 24.* **Courtyard** *9am-
5pm daily.* **Chapel** *1pm-6.30pm
Mon; 9am-6.30pm Tue, Fri; 9am-
6pm Sat, Sun.* **Map** *p72 J10.*

Hidden behind the buzzing Spui
square is a group of houses with
a history as lovely as its pristine
courtyard. Established in the 14th
century, the Begijnhof originally
provided modest homes for the
Beguines, a religious and (as
was the way in the Middle Ages
with religious establishments for
women) rather liberated sisterhood
of unmarried ladies from good
families, who, though not nuns and
thus taking no formal vows, lived
together in a close community and
had to take vows of chastity.

Since they did not have to take
vows of poverty, the Beguines were
free to dispose of their property as
they saw fit, further ensuring their
emancipation as a community.
They could, however, renounce
their vows at any moment and
leave – for instance, if they wanted
to get married. The last sister
died in 1971, while one of her
predecessors never left, despite
dying back in 1654. She was buried
in a 'grave in the gutter' under
a red granite slab that remains
visible – and is often adorned with
flowers – on the path.

Most of the neat little houses
around the courtyard were
modernised in the 17th and 18th
centuries. In the centre stands the
Engelse Kerk (English Reformed
Church), built as a church around
1400 and given over to Scottish
(no, really) Presbyterians living
in the city in 1607; many became
pilgrims when they decided to

travel further to the New World in search of religious freedom. Now one of the principal places of worship for Amsterdam's English community, the church is worth a look primarily to see the pulpit panels, designed by a young Mondrian.

Also in the courtyard is a **Catholic church**, secretly converted from two houses in 1665 following the complete banning of open Catholic worship after the Reformation. It once held the regurgitated Eucharist host that starred in the Miracle of Amsterdam, a story depicted in the church's beautiful stained-glass windows. There's an information centre next door. The house at no.34, known as the **Houtenhuis**, dates from 1475 and is the oldest wooden house still standing within the city.

While visiting the Begijnhof, be sure to check out the beautiful painted stones on the wall behind the Houtenhuis, each of which depicts a scene from the Bible. Dating from the 17th and 18th centuries, these stones, once housed in the Rijksmuseum's vaults, were restored and installed here in 1961.

In the know
When to visit

The courtyard entrance is easy to miss, but the site is a popular point for tours and is mentioned in various guidebooks so its hidden location doesn't always deter crowds. Visit first thing in the morning or just before it closes for the most room to roam the beautiful courtyard.

MR PORTER

Haesje Claes €€
Spuistraat 275 (624 9998, www. haesjeclaes.nl). Tram 1, 2, 5. **Open** *noon-midnight daily, last orders at 10pm.* **Map** *p72 J10* 9 *Dutch*
Between Dam Square and Spui, this beloved landmark is especially popular with tourists, though locals also come for traditional Dutch food, including *erwtensoep* (split-pea soup) and a great *stamppot* (potato mashed with greens). The service, however, is somewhat un-Dutch: friendly and fast. You can order from the same menu at the delightful brown bar next door at no.269, **Café de Koningshut**.

D'Vijff Vlieghen €€€€
Spuistraat 294-302 (530 4060, www.vijffvlieghen.nl). Tram 1, 2, 5. **Open** *6-10pm daily.* **Map** *p72 J10* 12 *Dutch*
'The Five Flies' achieves a rich Golden Age vibe – it even has a Rembrandt room, with etchings – but also works as a purveyor of over-the-top kitsch. The food is best described as poshed-up Dutch.

Vleminckx €
Voetboogsteeg 33 (vleminckxdesausmeester.nl). Tram 1, 2, 5. **Open** *noon-7pm Mon, Sun; 11am-7pm Tue-Wed, Fri-Sat; 11am-8pm Thur.* **Map** *p72 J11* 13 *Chip shop*
Chunky Belgian chips served with your choice of toppings. Opt for the *oorlog* ('war') version, where your chips are accompanied by a spicy peanut sauce, mayo and onions.

Bars

5&33
Martelaarsgracht 5 (820 5333, www.5and33.nl). Tram 1, 2, 4, 5, 9, 13, 16, 17, 24. **Open** *6.30am-1am Mon-Fri; 6.30am-2am Sat, Sun.* **Map** *p72 L7* 1
Red skull sculptures. Penis lamps. Projection curtains. It's hard to do over-the-top in a tasteful and welcoming manner, but the insanely arty Art'otel does just that with 5&33, its kitchen/bar/library/ lounge/art gallery, located across from Centraal Station. Drop in for a coffee or a Horny Mule cocktail and decide how long you want to linger.

Café de Dokter

*Rozenboomsteeg 4 (626 4427, www. cafe-de-dokter.nl). Tram 1, 2, 4, 5, 9, 13, 14, 16, 17, 24. **Open** 4pm-1am Wed-Sat. **Map** p72 J10* ④

The smallest bar in Amsterdam at just a handful of square metres, the Doctor is also one of the oldest, dishing out the cure for whatever ails you since 1798. Centuries of character and all kinds of gewgaws are packed into the extremely compact space. Whisky figures large (there's a monthly special) and snacks include smoked *osseworst* (cured sausage) with gherkins. If it's too cosy, then head one block north to the similarly old-school **De Engelse Reet** (Begijnensteeg 4, 623 1777).

Café Hoppe

*Spui 18-20 (420 4420, www.café-hoppe.nl). Tram 1, 2, 4, 5, 9, 14, 16, 24. **Open** 8am-1am Sun-Thur, Sun; 8am-2am Fri, Sat. **Map** p72 K7* ⑤

The bonvivant beer magnate Freddy Heineken (1923-2002) spent so much time in this ancient, woody watering hole that he ended up buying it. What appealed to Fred most about the place is that it catered to everyone, from students wanting a cheap *biertje*, through tourists enjoying the terrace, to suits stopping by after work. And nothing much has changed. If you want something more evocative of a classic Parisian brasserie, try **Café Luxembourg** next door.

♥ MR PORTER Amsterdam

*Spuistraat 175 (811 3399, www. mrportersteakhouse.com). Tram 1, 2, 5, 9, 13, 14, 16, 17. **Open** 7am-1am Mon-Thur, Sun; 7am-2am Fri, Sat. **Map** p72 J9* ⑨

Perched at the top of the W Hotel, MR PORTER is every bit a luxurious haven with breathtaking views of the skyline. In the summer, enjoy a Porters Americano – the house cocktail – as you dip your feet into the pool on the terrace. During winter, curl up with an espresso martini by the fire. Reservations can be made for the steakhouse restaurant online, but if you just want a drink and some nibbles (and not blow your budget), you generally won't have trouble getting a seat either inside or on the terrace. There's a sense of exclusivity, but everyone is welcome.

Coffeeshops

Abraxas

*Jonge Roelensteeg 12-14 (626 1317). Tram 1, 2, 5, 4, 9, 14, 16, 24. **Open** 8am-1am daily. **No cards**. **Map** p72 J9* ①

Located down a narrow alley, this lively shop is a tourist hotspot. Staff are friendly, the internet connection is free and chessboards are plentiful – as are the separate rooms connected by spiral staircases. It also has a healthy-sized drug menu, including half a dozen bio weeds and spacecakes.

Dampkring

*Handboogstraat 29 (638 0705). Tram 1, 2, 5. **Open** 10am-1am daily. **No cards**. **Map** p72 J11* ③

Known for its unforgettable (even by stoner standards) interior, the visual experience acquired from Dampkring's decor could make a mushroom trip look grey. Moulded walls and sculpted ceilings are painted auburn and laced with caramel-coloured wood panelling – which made it the perfect location for *Ocean's Twelve*.

Shops & services

Albert Heijn

*Nieuwezijds Voorburgwal 226 (421 8344, www.ah.nl). Tram 1, 2, 4, 5, 9, 13, 14, 16, 17, 24. **Open** 8am-10pm daily. **No cards**. **Map** p72 J9* ①

Food & drink

The Dutch have a very close relationship with this, their biggest supermarket brand. The monopoly it holds on the city means you're always within a stone's throw of a 'Bertie': be it a regular store, an 'AH XL', or small 'AH To Go'.

De Bierkoning

Paleisstraat 125 (625 2336, www. bierkoning.nl). Tram 1, 2, 4, 5, 9, 13, 14, 16, 17, 24. **Open** *11am-7pm Mon-Sat; 1-7pm Sun.* **Map** *p72 J9* ❷
Food & drink
Named in honour of its location behind the Royal Palace, the 'Beer King' stocks a head-spinning 1,200 brands of beer from around the world, and a range of fine glasses to sup from.

💗 Bij Ons Vintage

Nieuwezijds Voorburgwal 150 (06 1187 1278, www.bijons-vintage.nl). Tram 1, 2, 5, 13, 14, 17. **Open** *noon-7pm Mon; 11am-7pm Tue, Wed; 10am-9pm Thur; 10am-7pm Fri, Sat; noon-7pm Sun.* **Map** *p72 J8* ❸
Fashion
This place is rammed with leather jackets, woollen hats, old Polaroid cameras and even some authentic 1960s ottomans. There's so much random gear here you'll be struck with bargain-hunting fever.

Book Market at the Spui

Spui (www.deboekenmarktophetspui. nl). Tram 1, 2, 4, 5, 9, 16, 24. **Open** *10am-6pm Fri.* **Map** *p72 J10* ❹
Market
Every Friday, the Spui square is filled with antiquarian booksellers covering all subjects and languages – it's a browser's paradise.

HEMA

Kalverstraat 212 (422 8988, www. hema.nl). Tram 1, 2, 4, 5, 9, 14, 16, 24. **Open** *9am-7pm Mon-Wed, Fri, Sat; 9am-9pm Thur; 11am-6.30pm Sun.* **Map** *p72 K11* ❻ *Gifts & souvenirs*

A high-street institution, HEMA is the place to check out when you need just about anything – clothes, towels, notebooks, soap dispensers, ring binders, those little bike lights – you name it, HEMA's probably got it.

Entertainment

💗 Bitterzoet

Spuistraat 2 (421 2318, www. bitterzoet.com). Tram 1, 2, 5. **Open** *varies.* **Admission** *varies.* **No cards.** **Map** *p72 K7* ❷ *Club*
Casual and cosy, 'Bitter sweet' has been around for more than a decade. The key to its success is booking bands and DJs who do it more for the passion. Hip hop, street art, alternative rock, Afrobeat or broken beats may define particular nights – or mashed up together in a single night.

💗 Disco Dolly

Handboogstraat 11 (620 1779, www.discodolly.nl). Tram 1, 2, 4, 5, 9, 14, 16. **Open** *11pm-4am Mon-Thur, Sun; 11pm-5am Fri, Sat.* **Admission** *free-€10.* **No cards.** **Map** *p72 J10* ❸ *Club*
Disco Dolly doesn't stray too far from commercial disco, funk and house. If you feel old among the teen and early twenties clientele, try sister night bar **Bloemenbar**, next door at no.15.

Prik

Spuistraat 109 (320 0002, www. prikamsterdam.nl). Tram 1, 2, 5, 13, 17. **Open** *4pm-1am Mon-Thur; 4pm-3am Fri, Sun; 3pm-1am Sun.* **Map** *p72 J8* ❻ *Gay club*
This popular LGBT meeting point attracts a diverse bunch who enjoy Prik's 'lovely liquids, sexy snacks and twisted tunes'.

Grachtengordel

The UNESCO-listed Grachtengordel ('canal belt') forms
a horseshoe round the historical Old Centre. Singel was
the original medieval city moat, while other canals such
as Herengracht, Keizersgracht and Prinsengracht, which
follow its line outwards, were part of a Golden Age renewal
scheme for the rich. The connecting canals and streets,
originally home to workers and artisans, have a number of
cafés and shops. Smaller canals worth seeking out include
Leliegracht, Bloemgracht, Egelantiersgracht, Spiegelgracht
and Brouwersgracht.

We've split venues on the canals into two: Western
Canal Belt denotes the stretch of canals to the west and
north of Leidsestraat, taking in Leidseplein, whereas
Southern Canal Belt covers the area that lies to the east
and Rembrandtplein.

Must-see sights
Poignant insight into a personal history at Anne Frank Huis (p100) and explore the city's waterways on a canal cruise (p98).

Cutting-edge art
Foam (p110), a photography museum worth snapping at.

Shop till you drop
Nine Streets (p103), where high fashion meets cheese, and the bloomin' beautiful Bloemenmarkt (p111).

Cultural fix
Catch a film at art deco wonder, Pathé Tuschinski (p114), or visit Stadsschouwburg (p106) for world-class drama, dance and music.

Memorable dining
Guts & Glory's (p108) deliciously inventive menu and Tempo Doeloe (p108) for memorable Indonesian *rijsttafel*.

Best-stocked bars
Choose from around a hundred beers at Arendsnest (p101) and even more wines at Vyne (p102).

Best for gigs
Catch a band at Melkweg (p105) or Paradiso (p113) – two of the city's premier music venues.

Big night out
Anything goes at outrageous gay cruising club Church (p112), and R'n'B gets a bootylicious soundsystem at Jimmy Woo (p105).

Western Canal Belt

Prinsengracht is easily the most charming of the canals in this area. Pompous façades have mellowed as shady trees, cosy cafés and some of Amsterdam's more funkadelic houseboats have grown in number here. There's some good shopping to be had; further north, the smart **Nine Streets** linking Prinsengracht, Keizersgracht and Herengracht all offer a diverse mix of speciality shops for browsing.

On your way up Prinsengracht, the tall spire of the nearly 400-year-old **Westerkerk** rears into view. Its tower is the tallest structure in this part of town,

and climbing up it affords a good view of the **Anne Frank Huis**, now a museum of remembrance to the life of the diarist and other victims of the Holocaust. Fans of René Descartes – if you think, you therefore probably are – can pay tribute at his house around the corner at Westermarkt 6; while art-lovers can admire the interiors of the **Bijbels Museum**.

Leidseplein is the tourist centre of Amsterdam. It's packed with merrymakers drinking at cafés and is dominated by the Stadsschouwburg, along with many cinemas, theatres and restaurants. Max Euweplein offers a route to the greener pastures of Vondelpark.

→ Getting around
Trams 13, 14 and 17 run along Radhuisstraat through the heart of the Western Canal Belt. Canal bikes are available for hire from multiple tourist attractions throughout the Grachtengordel, including Anne Frank Huis; for details of canal cruises, see Canal Cruising, p98. If you prefer to stay on dry land, the Grachtengordel and surrounds is a great area to explore by foot. A stroll from Anne Frank Huis to Bloemenmarkt takes five to ten minutes, give or take a few stops for photo opportunities.

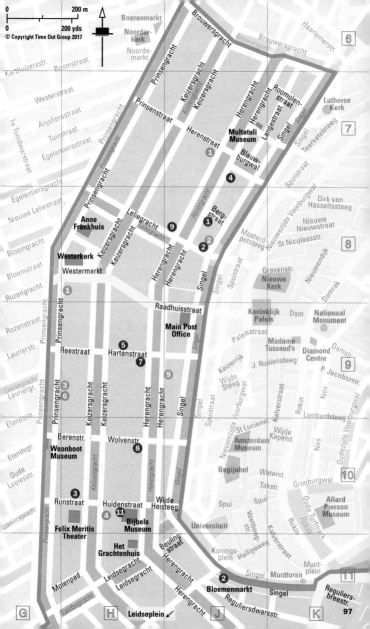

❤ Canal cruising

During a sojourn in the city, Hans Christian Andersen wrote, 'The view from my window, through the elms to the canal outside, is like a fairy tale.'

Canals are what people imagine when they think of Amsterdam, and they continue to enchant visitors today. Like any other city built on water, Amsterdam is best seen from a boat. The larger tourist boats, which can seat between 150 and 200 people and come complete with audio tour guides, are too big to squeeze through all of the narrow waterways connecting the Grachtengordel, but they still provide a doughty service past many of the World Heritage-listed highlights. You'll find the pick-up points for a lot of them along Stadhouderskade, which separates the Southern Canal Belt from the Museum Quarter and De Pijp. **Amsterdam Canal Cruises** (no.78, 679 1370, www. amsterdamcanalcruises.nl) collects from just outside the Heineken Brewery and offers a range of tours throughout the year, including a candle-lit evening cruise. **The Blue Boat Company** (no. 30, 679 1370, www.blueboat. nl) offers a similar service, including seasonal specials like the 'Water Colours Cruise' during the Amsterdam Light Festival (*see p64*). Prices range from €20 to €40 depending on the cruise type and time of year.

A bit further west along Stadhouderskade at no.11 is one of many pick-up and drop-off points for the **Canal Company** (217 0501, www.canal.nl). Here, you'll be able to jump on a variety of canal cruises, including a hop-on-hop-off canal bus. This service costs €21.50 for a 24-hour ticket and €24.50 for 48 hours. It takes you past key locations in the city including the Rijksmuseum (*see p130*) and Anne Frank Huis (*see p100*). Drop off and collection points are also at Rembrandt Square and Albert Cuypmarkt.

If you want to navigate the historical canals for yourself, you can also hire a canal bike for an hour or two at a time for €8 per person from the Canal Company. The bikes hold up to four people and you can pedal your way from Anne Frank Huis, Leidseplein or Rijksmuseum if you want a rest from pounding the pavements.

But if you'd prefer something with a bit more horsepower, powerboat rentals provide the best of both worlds. Companies including **Mokum Boot** (020 210 5700, mokumbootverhuur.nl), **Kin Boat** (020 261 3466, kinboat.com) and **Amsterdam Boat Centre** (020 428 2725, www.amsterdamboatcentre) hire boats from various locations throughout the city starting from €90 for two hours for up to eight people. No licence is required for boats less than 15 metres (50 foot) in length and some include a mini-fridge and barbecue hire. If you can get a group of four or more together, it's the perfect way to view Amsterdam's finest sights from the best seat in the house.

Bijbels Museum

Herengracht 366 (624 2436, www.bijbelsmuseum.nl). Tram 1, 2, 5. **Open** *11am-5pm Tue-Sun.* **Admission** *€8.50; €4.25 reductions; free under-4s, Iamsterdam.* **Map** *p97 H10.*
Housed in a restored 17th-century Vingboons canal house, the Bible Museum aims to illustrate life and worship with archaeological finds, models of ancient temples and a splendid collection of Bibles from several centuries (including a rhyming Bible from 1271). You can also admire the splendid Jacob de Wit paintings, and the grand garden with biblical plants.

Westerkerk

Prinsengracht 277-279 (624 7766, www.westerkerk.nl). Tram 13, 14, 17. **Open** *11am-4pm Mon-Fri; 1 April-1 Nov 11am-4pm Mon-Fri, 11am-3pm Sat. Services 10.30am Sun and Christmas Day.* **Admission** *free; Tower Tours €7.50. No cards.* **Map** *p97 H8.*
Before noise pollution, it was said that if you heard the bells of Westerkerk's tower, dating from 1631, you were in the Jordaan. The tower also offers a great view of this neighbourhood, provided you don't suffer from vertigo: the 85m (278ft) structure sways by 3cm in a good wind. The tower is emblazoned with a gaudy red, blue and gold 'XXX' crown; this was granted to the city in 1489 by the Holy Roman Emperor Maximillian in gratitude for the treatment he received during a pilgrimage to Amsterdam. The triple-X came to be used by local traders – and later by local pornographers – to denote quality, and is now on the city's flag and coat of arms. The church features a wide range of lunch and evening concerts, many free of charge.

💙 Anne Frank Huis

*Prinsengracht 267 (556 7105, www.annefrank.nl). Tram 13, 14, 17. **Open** Apr-Oct 9am-10pm daily. Nov-Mar, 9am-7pm daily. **Admission** €9; €4 reductions with 50c surcharge when booking online. Free under-9s. Online tickets sell out fast. **Map** p97 H8.*

During World War II, the young Jewish diarist Anne Frank and her family hid for two years behind a bookcase in the back annexe of this 17th-century canal house. During this time, young Anne kept a vivid diary, which is as confronting as it is emotionally compelling. The diary became a best friend of sorts for Anne, in which she wrote short stories and shared the details of her life in hiding. On 4 August 1944, the occupants were arrested and transported to concentration camps, where Anne died with her sister Margot and their mother. Her father, Otto, was the only one of eight to survive, and decided that Anne's diary should be published.

After the war the secret annex was on the list of buildings to be knocked down, but thanks to a number of campaigners, the house remained. The foundation, now known as the Anne Frank Huis, was set up and the rest is history: Anne's dream of becoming a best-selling author was fulfilled, with tens of millions of copies having since been printed in 70 languages. Today, more than a million visitors every year come to witness these sober rooms, which have been preserved throughout the decades. A new wing not only tells the story of Anne's family and the persecution of Jews, but also presents the difficulties of fighting discrimination of all types.

The museum is now one of the most popular in Amsterdam, so be prepared – booking online will save you a lot of time. Between 9am and 3.30pm the museum is only open to visitors with an online ticket for a certain timeslot, and tickets are available online exactly two months in advance. If your visit is a little more spontaneous, you can purchase tickets on the day from 3.30pm, but the line often extends past the Westerkerk and can take hours.

Woonboot Museum

Prinsengracht, opposite no.296 (427 0750, www.houseboatmuseum.nl). Tram 13, 14, 17. **Open** *Mar-Oct 10am-5pm daily. Nov-Feb 10am-5pm Tue-Sun. Closed last 3wks Jan and public holidays.* **Admission** *€4.50; €3.50 reductions, Iamsterdam. No cards.* **Map** *p97 H10.*

Aside from some discreet explanatory panels, a small slide show and a ticket clerk, the Hendrika Maria Houseboat Museum is laid out as a houseboat would be, to help visitors imagine what it's like to live on the water. It's more spacious than you might expect and does a good job of selling the lifestyle afforded by its unique comforts.

Restaurants & cafés

Bistro Bij Ons €€

Prinsengracht 287 (627 9016, www.bistrobijons.nl). Tram 13, 14, 17. **Open** *10am-midnight Tue-Sun.* **Map** *p97 H8* **❶** *Dutch*

In the shadow of the Westerkerk, two archetypal Amsterdam hostesses serve typical Dutch fare (think vegetable soup with meatballs, grandma's traditional *stamppot* mash, and warm apple pie) in a canal house restaurant with a living-room vibe and watery views.

Caffé il Momento €

Singel 180 (336 652, www.caffeilmomento.nl). Tram 1, 2, 5, 13, 17. **Open** *8am-6pm Mon-Fri; 9am-6pm Sat, Sun.* **Map** *p97 J8* **❷** *Café*

The inside of this quaint café is just as charming as its exterior would have you believe. Grab a coffee to go or linger at one of the cosy tables along the exposed brick walls. The food always delicious and the owner is also super-friendly.

Envy €€€

Prinsengracht 381 (344 6407, www.envy.nl). Tram 13, 14, 17. **Open** *6pm-1am Mon-Thur; noon-3pm and 6pm-1am Fri-Sun.* **Map** *p97 H9* **❸** *Italian*

A designer deli-cum-restaurant serving an arsenal of delicacies, which emerge from the streamlined refrigerators that line the walls, and from the able kitchen staff. The perfect place for those times when you want to try a bit of everything. A few doors down is sister establishment **Vyne** (*see p102*) which is more of a wine bar, with a menu of quality nibbles.

Lotti's €€€

Herengracht 255 (888 5500, www.lottis.com). Tram 1, 2, 5, 13, 14, 17. **Open** *7am-midnight Sun-Wed; 7am-1am Thur-Sat.* **Map** *p97 J9* **❾** *Bar/restaurant*

Boasting a prime location on the picturesque Herengracht, Lotti's café, bar and grill serves everything from seafood to steak, with various good things in between. Owned by the prestigious Soho House group, the restaurant is dripping in chic style. By day, you'll spot the city's hipsters tapping away on their laptops, but by night it's a buzzing after-work bar. For the ultimate sugar hit, try the brownie.

Bars

♥ Arendsnest

Herengracht 90 (421 2057, www.arendsnest.nl). Tram 1, 2, 5, 13, 14, 17. **Open** *noon-midnight Sun-Thur; noon-2am Fri, Sat.* **Map** *p97 J7* **❶**

A temple to the humble hop, and set in a lovely canal house, the 'Eagle's Nest' sells only Dutch beer. There's 52 beers on tap and 100 bottled beers, from pale ale to smoked porter. Arendsnest also serves excellent cheese and sausage snacks.

Korte Leidsedwarsstraat

Café Eijlders

Korte Leidsedwarsstraat 47 (624 2704, www.cafeeijlders.com). Tram 1, 2, 5, 7, 10, 14. **Open** *4.30pm-1am Mon-Wed; noon-1am Thur; noon-2am Fri, Sat; noon-1am Sun.* **Map** *p109 G12* ❸

Neon tat on one side, trendy Wendys on the other; Eijlders on Leidseplein is a cerebral alternative to both. A meeting place for the Resistance during the war, it now has a boho feel, with exhibitions, poetry nights and music – sometimes jazz, sometimes classical. Decor is handsome, with stained glass and dark wood.

Café de Pels

Huidenstraat 25 (622 9037, www. cafedepels.nl). Tram 1, 2, 5. **Open** *9am-1am Sun-Thur; 9am-3am Fri, Sat.* **No cards.** **Map** *p97 H10* ❹

The Nine Streets are littered with characterful bars, and this one is a lovely old-style, tobacco-stained example that has an intellectual bent. In fact, Café de Pels can justifiably claim a prime spot in Amsterdam's literary and political legacy: writers, journalists and social activists often meet at this erstwhile Provo hangout to chew the fat – although it's a nice spot in which to relax, whatever your mood.

♥ Vyne

Prinsengracht 411 (244 6408, www.vyne.nl). Tram 13, 14, 17. **Open** *6pm-midnight Mon-Thur; 5pm-1am Fri, Sat; 4-11pm Sun.* **Map** *p97 H9* ❻

If you enjoyed designer deli-cum-restaurant **Envy** (*see* p101) and appreciate a decent drop, you'll do well to stop by Vyne. The dimly lit wine bar is the sister of Envy. The place stocks over 270 varieties of wine and also serves light nibbles to help you stay on your chair after all the tastings. The atmosphere is self-described as 'modern brown café'.

Coffeeshops

Amnesia

Herengracht 133 (427 7874). Tram 13, 14, 17. **Open** *9.30am-1am daily.* **No cards.** **Map** *p97 J8* ❶

You have to wonder at the choice of name, but Amnesia is a shop with swank decor, comfortable cushions and deep red walls. Located off the main tourist routes, it's often cool and quiet. The pre-rolled joints are strong and smokeable. Summer time brings outdoor seating to the large, quiet canal street.

💜 Nine Streets

Between Westermarkt and Leidsegracht. Tram 1, 2, 5. **Map p97 H9**

There are few places in the world that can combine fishnets, cheese and high fashion with seamless, albeit haphazard, ease, but De Negen Straatjes (the Nine Streets) manage to pull it off with picture-perfect charm. Affectionately dubbed 'Negens', these parallel streets connect the city's three main canals between Raadhuisstraat and Leidsegracht. The cobbled streets are steeped in both style and history, constructed in the first half of the 17th century when the canals of the Grachtengordel were dug out around the medieval town to cater for its growing population.

Fast forward over 400 years, the area is a thriving cultural hub of cafés, restaurants, galleries and hundreds of retailers, for which De Negen Straatjes is best known. From cheesemongers to doll repairs to designer retailers – the area has something for everyone. First stop has to be that vortex of vintage, **Laura Dols**, a fashionable cavern that positively glitters. True Dutch style can be cashed in at **Hester van Eeghen**, the shop of the celebrated local shoe designer. Known for her way with leather, Hester loves a geometric shape or two and brash colours. **Exota** – not to be confused with stores that sell fluffy handcuffs – is one for women and kids. Thick-knit bright scarves adorn the wooden shelves in winter, while dainty frocks and denim will always be a big draw in the summer. Despite its bumbling name, **Relaxed at Home** is a bright and airy store that's the sartorial equivalent of a cuddle – think thick nude scarves by Dutch stalwart Scotch & Soda.

If you have serious shopping stamina and haven't quenched your consumer thirst at the end of peering into every window of the Nine Streets, there are a few other similar streets: connecting Herenstraat and Prinsenstraat in the Western Canal Belt, and Hazenstraat in the Jordaan.

▶ *For details of the shops mentioned here, see pp104-105.*

Grey Area

Oude Leliestraat 2 (420 4301, www. greyarea.nl). Tram 1, 2, 5, 13, 14, 17. **Open** *noon-8pm daily.* **No cards.** **Map** *p97 J8* ❷

Run by two blokes living the modern American dream: running a thriving Amsterdam coffeeshop that offers some of the best weed and hash on the planet (try the Bubble Gum or Grey Mist Crystals). Also on offer are large glass bongs, a vaporiser and free refills of organic coffee. The owners are very affable and often more baked than the patrons; sometimes they stay in bed and miss opening time.

Shops & services

The Darling

Runstraat 4 (422 3142, www. thedarlingamsterdam.com). Tram 1, 2, 5. **Open** *1-6pm Mon; 11am-6pm Tue-Sat; noon-6pm Sun.* **Map** *p97 H10* ❸ *Lifestyle*

Quirky designer Nadine van der Zee set up shop here in 2009. The shop offers an eclectic mix of clothing, jewellery, accessories and lifestyle products all 'made with love'. It also hosts monthly mini markets, live expos and shop nights.

Deco Sauna

Herengracht 115 (623 8215, www. saunadeco.nl). Tram 1, 2, 5, 13, 17. **Open** *noon-11pm Mon, Wed-Sat; 3-11pm Tue; 1-7pm Sun.* **Admission** *from €19 in summer.* **Map** *p97 J7* ❹ *Health & beauty*

This beautiful art deco sauna provides facilities for a Turkish bath, Finnish sauna and cold plunge bath. There's also a solarium. Massages and skincare treatments are all available by appointment. Mixed bathing only.

Exota

Hartenstraat 10-13 (344 9390, www.exota.com). Tram 1, 2, 5, 13, 17. **Open** *10.30am-6.30pm Mon-Fri; 10am-6pm Sat; noon-6pm Sun.* **Map** *p97 H9* ❺ *Vintage*

Quirky vintage store Exota began selling 'first-class second-hand', before owners Ann and George started making their own vintage-oriented knitwear under the King Louie label. The brand is now stocked worldwide, but it began right here in Amsterdam.

Hester van Eeghen

Hartenstraat 37 (626 9211, https:// hestervaneeghen.com). Tram 1, 2, 5, 13, 17. **Open** *1-6pm Mon; 11am-6pm Tue-Sat; noon-5pm Sun.* **Map** *p97 H9* ❼ *Accessories*

With a dazzling array of accessories, shoes and infamous bags, this shop is a perfect point of call for a special and unique gift you can't replicate in an airport store. The thousands of colours and hundreds of models are the handy work of talented Dutch designer Hester van Eeghen.

Laura Dols

Wolvenstraat 7 (624 9066, www. lauradols.nl). Tram 1, 2, 5. **Open** *11am-6pm Mon-Wed, Fri, Sat; 11am-7pm Thur; noon-6pm Sun.* **Map** *p97 H10* ❽ *Fashion*

When Jean Paul Gaultier, Viktor & Rolf and Susan Sarandon regularly pop into your store, you know you're on to something good. This place is jam-packed with 1950s-style wedding, ballroom and Hollywood glitter gear.

Otherist

Leliegracht 6 (320 0420, www. otherist.com). Tram 13, 14, 17. **Open** *noon-6pm Wed-Sat; noon-5pm Sun.* **Map** *p97 J8* ❾ *Gifts & souvenirs*

If you are out to stock your own cabinet of curiosities or looking for the ultimate gift, The Otherist is alternative-shopping heaven:

Stadsschouwburg p106

glass eyeballs, 'vegan mini-skulls', butterfly specimens, amulets, hip flasks, medical posters and an ever-changing selection of other curiosa and handmade design items.

Relaxed at Home
Huidenstraat 19 (320 2001, www. theninestreets.com/relaxed-at-home.html). Tram 1, 2, 5. **Open** *noon-6pm Mon, Sun; 10am-6pm Tue-Sat.* **Map** *p97 H10* ⓫ *Fashion*
The versatile store owners of Relaxed at Home have made theirs a true one-stop-shop, stocking everything from clothing and fashion accessories to interior design gems – including furniture and paintings. A great place to indulge in a bit of retail therapy after history-heavy sightseeing. For more on the Nine Streets, *see* p103.

Entertainment

DeLaMar Theater
Marnixstraat 402 (0900 335 2627 €1 each, www.delamar.nl). Tram 1, 2, 5, 7, 10. **Box office** *by phone noon-7.30pm Mon-Fri. In person 4pm-5pm daily; until start of show on performance days. Tickets prices vary.* **Map** *p109 G12* ⑥ *Theatre*
The luxurious DeLaMar hosts major musicals, opera and drama. Its two auditoria can accommodate 600 and 900 people respectively,

making it a key destination in the Leidseplein theatre district.

💜 Jimmy Woo
Korte Leidsedwarsstraat 18 (626 3150, www.jimmywoo.com). Tram 1, 2, 5, 7, 10. **Open** *11pm-3am Thur, Sun; 11pm-4am Fri, Sat.* **Admission** *varies.* **Map** *p109 G12* ⑨ *Club*
Amsterdam had never seen anything quite so luxuriously cosmopolitan as Jimmy Woo, when it first opened. Marvel at the lounge filled with a mix of modern and antique furniture, and confirm for yourself the merits of the bootylicious light design and sound system. If you have problems getting inside, try the equally hip and happening **Chicago Social Club** (Leidseplein 12, 760 1171, www.chicagosocialclub.

💜 Melkweg
Lijnbaansgracht 234A (531 8181, www.melkweg.nl). Tram 1, 2, 5, 7, 10. **Open** *daily until late.* **Admission** *€5-€32. Membership (compulsory) €4/mth; €25/yr.* **Map** *p109 G12* ⑩ *Live music*
The Melkweg was a milking factory in its past life, hence its name, which translates as 'Milky Way'. The venue is operated by a non-profit group of artists who have run it since 1970. It hosts events

Museum Willet-Holthuysen

with music of all styles, so draws an eclectic crowd. Its two decent-sized concert halls – the Max room has a capacity of up to 1,500 – offer a full programme year round. It also has an excellent cinema, gallery and a café, and books more intimate shows across the street at **Sugar Factory** (627 0008, www.sugarfactory.nl). Don't fret about the compulsory membership – you can purchase it at the same time as booking.

♥ Stadsschouwburg

Leidseplein 26 (624 2311, www. stadsschouwburgamsterdam.nl). Tram 1, 2, 5, 7, 10. **Box office** *noon-6pm Mon-Sat; from 2hrs before performance Sun. Tickets prices vary.* **Map** *p109 G12* ⑪ *Theatre*
Situated centrally in Leidseplein, the striking 19th-century municipal theatre is the chief subsidised venue for drama, dance and music, featuring work by local companies and touring ensembles. It's also home to **Toneelgroep Amsterdam** (795 9900, tga.nl/en), the biggest and boldest repertory company in the Netherlands. Thursday evening performances have English surtitles. The Stadsschouwburg has two stages. There's also a fine café, **Stravinsky**, and a well-stocked theatre and film bookshop.

Southern Canal Belt

The Southern Canal Belt's main square is **Rembrandtplein** – unashamedly tacky and home to an array of tasteless (and worse) establishments, ranging from traditional striptease parlours to even seedier modern peepshow joints and nondescript cafés. Fortunately, there are a few exceptions to the prevailing tawdriness – the grand **Café Restaurant De Kroon** (no.17-I), art deco building **Schiller** (no.26), and

HL de Jong's eclectic masterpiece, the **Pathé Tuschinski** on Reguliersbreestraat. Also nearby is the floating flower market at the southern tip of Singel (the **Bloemenmarkt**).

From the square, walk south along shopping and eating street Utrechtsestraat, or explore the picturesque Reguliersgracht and Amstelveld. Whichever you choose, you'll cross **Herengracht** on your journey. As the first canal to be dug in the glory days, Herengracht attracted the richest of merchants and is still home to the most overblown houses on any of Amsterdam's canals.

The stretch built between Leidsestraat and Vijzelstraat is known as the **Golden Bend**. Around the corner on Vijzelstraat is the highly imposing **Stadsarchief** (City Archive). Nearby on Keizersgracht is the cutting-edge photography museum **Foam**.

Sights & museums

Museum van Loon
Keizersgracht 672 (624 5255, www.museumvanloon.nl). Tram 16, 24. **Open** *10am-5pm daily.* **Admission** *€9; €7 reductions; free under-6s, Iamsterdam. No cards.* **Map** *p109 K12.*
Few interiors of Amsterdam's grand canal houses have been preserved in anything approaching their original state, but the former van Loon residence is one that has. Designed by Adriaan Dortsman, it was originally the home of artist Ferdinand Bol. Hendrik van Loon bought it in 1884 and it was opened as a museum in 1973. The terrifically grand mid-18th-century interior and Louis XIV and XV decor is a delight. So is the art. There's a collection of family portraits from the 17th to the 20th centuries, and a modern art show every two years.

Museum Willet-Holthuysen
Herengracht 605 (523 1822, www. willetholthuysen.nl). *Tram 4, 9, 14.* **Open** *10am-5pm daily.* **Admission** *€9; €4.50-€7 reductions; free under-4s, Iamsterdam.* **Map** *p109 L11.*
This 17th-century mansion was purchased in the 1850s by the Willet-Holthuysen family. When Abraham, remembered as 'the Oscar Wilde of Amsterdam', died in 1889, his wife Sandrina Louisa, a hermaphrodite, left the house and its contents to the city on the condition it was preserved and opened as a museum. The family followed the fashion of the time and decorated it in the neo-Louis XVI style: it's densely furnished, with an impressive collection of rare objets d'art, glassware, silver, fine china and paintings.

Stadsarchief Amsterdam
Vijzelstraat 32 (251 1511, www. amsterdam.nl/stadsarchief). Tram 16, 24. **Open** *10am-5pm Tue-Fri; noon-5pm Sat, Sun.* **Admission** *free.* **Map** *p109 K12.*
The city archives are located in a decorative 1926 building that's shrouded in esoteric mystery. The highly ornate structure was designed by architect KPC de Bazel, a practitioner of Theosophy – a spiritualist movement. The grand centrepiece is the Treasure Room. As embellished as Tutankhamun's Tomb, it displays the prizes of the collection. The archives also host exhibitions and film screenings. There is an excellent bookstore and café.

Restaurants & cafés

Greenwoods €
Keizersgracht 465 (420 4330). Tram 1, 2, 5, 13, 17. **Open** *9.30am-6pm Mon-Thur; 9.30am-7pm Fri-Sun.* **Map** *p109 H11* ④ *Café*

Service at this teashop is friendly but can be slow. Everything is freshly made, though – cakes, scones and muffins are baked daily on the premises – so it's understandable. In summer, sit on the terrace by the canal for the ultimate alfresco eating experience.

♥ Guts & Glory €€€

Utrechtsestraat 6 (362 0030, www. gutsglory.nl). Tram 4, 9,14. **Open** *noon-3pm, 6-10pm daily.* **Map** *p109 L11* ⑤ *International*
If you fancy a meal with a side of surprise, Guts & Glory should be your first point of call. The versatile bar/restaurant offers a surprise set menu with six 'chapters', each inspired by a different culture or country. The chapters cover chicken, fish, vegetables, beef and pork. Its sister restaurant at Singel 210, **Breda** (622 5233, www.breda-amsterdam.com) has an innovative menu for serious foodies.

Japan Inn €

Leidsekruisstraat 4 (620 4989, www.japaninn.nl). Tram 1, 2, 5, 7, 10. **Open** *5-11pm daily.* **Map** *p109 H12* ⑥ *Japanese*
Japan Inn offers both quality and quantity. The fresh sushi and sashimi are served from the open kitchen and are a hit with students (who dig the quantity) and Japanese tourists (who come for the quality).

Lion Noir €€€

Reguliersdwarsstraat 28 (627 6603, www.lionnoir.nl). Tram 1, 2, 5. **Open** *noon-1am Mon-Thur; noon-3am Fri; 6pm-3am Sat; 6pm-1am Sun.* **Map** *p109 J11* ⑦ *French*
The emphasis at Lion Noir is on meat, with hearty but not overwhelming mains, including top-notch foie gras and duck breast medallions. The velvet and artfully weather-beaten leather furnishings, stuffed birds and (yes) ornamental dog skeletons, combined with the genetically perfect staff, give the impression of an Abercrombie & Fitch shoot curated by Tim Burton.

Los Pilones €€

Kerkstraat 63 (320 4651, www. lospilones.com). Tram 1, 2, 5. **Open** *4-midnight daily.* **Map** *p109 H12* ⑧ *Mexican*
A splendid Mexican cantina with an anarchic bent, Los Pilones is run by three young and friendly Mexican brothers, one of whom does the cooking, so expect authentic food rather than standard Tex-Mex fare.

Stach Food €

Nieuwe Spiegelstraat 52 (737 2679, www.stach-food.nl). Tram 7, 10. **Open** *8am-10pm daily.* **Map** *p109 J12* ⑩ *Sandwiches*
A healthy takeaway shop on the antique and art gallery strip. Sandwiches, salads and full meals – with a tiny coffee bar in the back.

♥ Tempo Doeloe €€€

Utrechtsestraat 75 (625 6718, www. tempodoeloerestaurant.nl). Tram 4. **Open** *6pm-midnight Mon-Sat.* **Map** *p109 L12* ⑪ *Indonesian*
This cosy and rather classy Indonesian restaurant (heck, it even has white linen) is widely thought to serve the city's best and spiciest *rijsttafel* ('rice table'), a local speciality, and not without good reason. It's best to book ahead; if you turn up on the off-chance and find the place full, try the much cheaper and more casual **Rice & Spice Asian Deli** and tea bar across the way (Utrechtsestraat 98A, 752 9772, www.riceandspice.nl).

Van Dobben €

Korte Reguliersdwarsstraat 5-9 (624 4200, www. eetsalonvandobben.nl). Tram 4, 9, 14, 16, 24. **Open** *9am-9pm Mon-Wed; 10am-1am Thur; 10am-2am Fri, Sat; 10.30am-8pm Sun.* **No cards.** **Map** *p109 K11* ⑫ *Dutch*

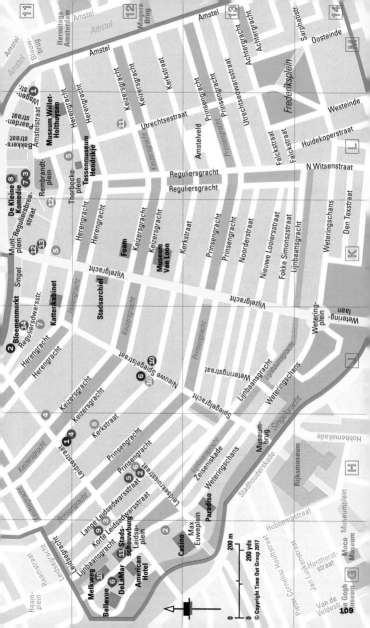

💙 Foam

Keizersgracht 609 (551 6500, www. foam.org). Tram 16, 24. **Open** *10am-6pm Mon-Wed, Sat, Sun; 10am-9pm Thur, Fri.* **Admission** *€10; €6-€7.50 reductions; free under-12s, Iamsterdam.* **Map** *p109 K12.*

In comparison to the big tourist magnets Rijksmuseum (*see* p130) and the Van Gogh Museum (*see* p137), which welcome millions of visitors through their doors every year, Foam – which has 200,000 annual visitors – is relatively small. But what it lacks in size it makes up for with the high quality of its exhibited talent.

Located in a tightly renovated 150-year-old canal house, the museum displays everything from still photography to interactive and immersive installations. And don't be fooled by its narrow exterior, Foam's interior is characterised by an effortless combination of original architecture and modern chrome and glass. Large white walls highlight the power of the exhibits over the jam-packed three floors.

Foam's programme rotates on a regular basis – typically every two to four months – and features a comprehensive array of talent, from rising local stars like Viviane Sassen to big names, including Diane Arbus and Chinese contemporary artist and activist Ai Weiwei, who captured the reality of modern-day refugees with an iPhone for his 2016 #SafePassage exhibition.

The museum sells limited-edition photographs, organises workshops and also publishes its own magazine. It collaborates with MTV each year to champion burgeoning creative talent. If you're feeling peckish, the basement café's food is a feast for the eyes as well as the stomach.

▶ *Check the website for details of exhibitions, free guided tours and pop-ups in other locations.*

Jasper Groen

A *kroket* is the national version of a croquette: a melange of meat and potato with a crusty, deep-fried skin, best served on a bun with lots of hot mustard. This 1945-era late-nighter is the uncontested champion of *kroket* shops.

Bars

De Balie
Kleine Gartmanplantsoen 10 (553 5151, www.debalie.nl). Tram 1, 2, 5, 7, 10. **Open** *9am-1am Mon-Thur; 9am-3am Fri; 10am-3am Sat; 10am-1am Sun.* **Map** *p109 G12* ❷
Theatre, new media, photography, cinema and literary events sit alongside lectures, debates and discussions about social and political issues at this influential centre for the local intelligentsia. Throw in a café too, and you've got healthy food for both mind and body.

Door 74
Reguilersdwarsstraat 741 (63 404 5122, www.door-74.com). Tram 4, 16, 24. **Open** *8pm-3am Sun-Thur, Sun; 8pm-4am Fri, Sat.* **Map** *p109 K11* ❺
'Exclusivity' may be a dirty word in Amsterdam's strenuously egalitarian bar scene, but rather than using inflated prices, long queues or grumpy doormen as its filter, Door 74 employs secrecy – and rewards in-the-know trendies with excellent cocktails mixed by some of the best barmen in the business. Make a reservation via text or online to guarantee entry into the unassuming-looking bar.

Shops & services

Art Unlimited
Keizersgracht 510 (624 8419, www.artnl.com). Tram 1, 2, 5. **Open** *noon-6pm Mon, Sun; 10.15am-6pm Tue-Sat.* **Map** *p109 H11* ❶ *Gifts & souvenirs*

The most comprehensive collection of international photographs and posters in the Netherlands, and the largest collection of postcards in Western Europe. The typography posters are good for tourists seeking a unique memento.

♥ Bloemenmarkt
Singel, between Muntplein & Koningsplein. Tram 1, 2, 4, 5, 9, 14, 16, 24. **Open** *9am-5.30pm Mon-Sat; 11am-5.30pm Sun.* **No cards. Map** *p109 J11* ❷ *Market*
This fascinating collage of colour is the world's only floating flower market, with 15 florists and garden shops (although many also hawk cheesy souvenirs these days) permanently ensconced on barges along the southern side of Singel. The plants and flowers usually last well and are good value.

Gilian Originals
Nieuwe Spiegelstraat 46 (260 0662, www.gilianoriginals.nl). Tram 7, 10. **Open** *11am-5.30pm Tue-Sat.* **Map** *p109 J12* ❻ *Jewellery*
This unique jewellery store features original works with a bohemian flavour: bracelets, earings, necklaces and rings. High-quality products – including gold and rare stones – are used, but the prices won't break the bank.

Public House of Art
Nieuwe Spiegelstraat 39 (221 3680, www.publichouseofart.com). Tram 7, 10. **Open** *noon-7pm Sun, Mon; 10am-7pm Tue-Sat.* **Map** *p109 J12* ❿ *Art*
Art enthusiasts eat your hearts out. The makers of this creative paradise believe 'art is for all – to disrupt not bankrupt'. Remarkable photography, digital art and paintings are available here, starting at €100 per print. It works in four price tiers – house, villa, mansion and castle – to suit all budgets.

AIR

Amstelstraat 16 (820 0670, www.air.nl). Tram 9, 14. **Open** *11pm-4am Thur; 11pm-5am Fri, Sat; 11.30pm-4am Sun.* **Admission** *€10-€15.* **Map** *p109 M11* **1** *Club*

Like a phoenix from the ashes, AIR Amsterdam rose from the remains of legendary club iT. The musical offerings are varied, and the crowd mixed. House and funk prevail at De Nachtbar on Thursday; Friday often has a techno feel; on Saturday, it's all a bit more commercial.

Bourbon Street

Leidsekruisstraat 6-8, Leidseplein (623 3440, www.bourbonstreet.nl). Tram 1, 2, 5, 7, 10. **Open** *10pm-4am Mon-Thur, Sun; 10pm-5am Fri, Sat.* **Admission** *€3-€10; free Mon, Tue, Sun; before 11pm Wed, Thur; before 10.30pm Fri, Sat.* **Map** *p109 H12* **2** *Live music*

In the heart of the tourist area, this blues club has a spacious bar and a late licence. Musicians are welcome at the regular jam sessions, and international acts drop by at least a couple of times a week. It's by no means a glamorous venue, but if late-night music played live is your thing, you won't be disappointed.

Claire

Rembrandtplein 17 (www.claire.nl). Tram 4, 9, 14. **Open** *11pm-4am Thur; Fri-Sat 11pm-8am.* **Admission** *varies.* **Map** *p109 L11* **3** *Club*

The successor of Amsterdam's iconic Studio 80, Claire is the self-described 'best friend, affair and archrival' of the city's nocturnal creatures. The club, which debuted a stellar line-up during Amsterdam Dance Event (ADE) in 2016, is co-owned by Juri Miralles and Marlon Arfman, who also have a hand in Disco Dolly (*see* p94).

♥ Club Church

Kerkstraat 52 (www.clubchurch.nl). Tram 1, 2, 5, 7, 10. **Open** *8pm-1am Tue, Wed; 10pm-4am Thur; 10pm-5am Fri, Sat; 4pm-8pm Sun.* **Admission** *varies.* **Map** *p109 H12* **4** *Gay club*

Sex is unambiguously on the agenda in this cavernous gay venue. Erotic theme nights run the full gamut of (mostly male) pervy possibility. Several of the city's fetish parties have also migrated here. To top it all, Church features a bar with Greek-style columns, a stage perfect for drag-queen acts, a great sound and light system, and various dark, dark chambers.

Club Up/De Kring

Korte Leidsedwarsstraat 26 (623 6985, www.clubup.nl). Tram 1, 2, 5, 7, 10. **Open** *11pm- 4am Thur; 11pm-5am Fri, Sat.* **Admission** *€5-€25.* **Map** *p109 H12* **5** *Club*

Club Up is an intimate venue with a great sound system, connected via a corridor to artists' members' club De Kring. If you can, visit when both areas are accessible, since De Kring provides the laid-back atmosphere that the often-packed, discotheque-like ballroom of Club Up lacks. DJs spin disco, techno and house.

Escape

Rembrandtplein 11 (622 1111, www.escape.nl). Tram 4, 9, 14. **Open** *11pm-4am Thur, Sun; 11pm-5am Fri, Sat.* **Admission** *€5-€20.* **No cards.** **Map** *p109 L11* **7** *Club*

With a capacity of 2,000, this is as big as clubbing gets in central Amsterdam, and is popular with a younger, more mainstream crowd. It attracts queues on Saturday and Sunday evenings, and the bouncers are wary of groups of tourists, so slap on some hair product and get in line early.

❤ Paradiso

*Weteringschans 6-8, Southern
Canal Belt (626 4521, www.
paradiso.nl). Tram 1, 2, 5, 7, 10.
Open 7pm-late daily, depending
on event. **Admission** varies. **Map**
p109 H13*

Amsterdam's prime music venue,
Paradiso is housed in a former
church. Fitting, then, that it's
now known as the city's 'temple
of pop'. As is generally the case
with iconic music hubs, Paradiso's
foundations tell a colourful story.

In 1968 'Cosmic Relaxation
Center Paradiso' opened to create
an open platform for burgeoning
creative talent. The name Paradiso
soon became synonymous with
counterculture and cutting-
edge rock music (and, perhaps
inevitably, soft drugs).

The years that followed saw
countless up-and-coming artists
and enthusiastic audiences
squeeze through its doors. Almost
50 years later, Paradiso has

secured its place as a pop podium
and cultural hub for national and
international audiences. Its stage
has been graced by hundreds of
rock, soul, country and pop music
legends. Iconic influencers such
as Al Green and Smokey Robinson
have brought the house down,
and the venue has also helped
pave the way for the likes of Franz
Ferdinand, Kings of Leon and the
White Stripes. With large stained-
glass windows and high ceilings,
the building still displays its grand
origins. In addition to the main
hall, which has a capacity of 1,500,
the venue showcases independent
and break-through talent in a
smaller room upstairs.

Paradiso also hosts fashion
shows, classical ensembles and
even the occasional lecture. The
music venue and club nights are
most popular, however, and tickets
sell quickly, so check the website
in advance if you want to see one
of your favourite acts.

GRACHTENGORDEL

De Kleine Komedie

Amstel 56-58 (624 0534, www.
dekleinekomedie.nl). Tram 4, 9, 14,
16, 24. Box office 4-6pm or until
start of performance Mon-Sat.
Tickets €9-€25. Map p109 L11 ⑧
Theatre

Built in 1786, De Kleine Komedie
is Amsterdam's oldest theatre and
still one of its most important.
Extremely popular with locals, it's
one of the city's most colourful
venues as well as the nation's pre-
eminent cabaret and music stage.

Pathé de Munt

Vijzelstraat 15 (0900 1458 premium
rate, www.pathe.nl). Tram 4, 9, 14,
16. Screens 13. Tickets €5-€10.50.
Map p109 K11 ⑫ *Cinema*

This is central Amsterdam's
monster multiplex. In its favour
are huge screens and comfortable
seating, making it the best choice
in the city centre for big-budget
Hollywood kicks.

♥ Pathé Tuschinski

Reguliersbreestraat 26-34 (0900
1458 premium rate, www.pathe.nl).
Tram 4, 9, 14, 16. Screens 6. Tickets
€5-€10.50. Map p109 K11 ⑬ *Cinema*

This extraordinary cinema is
named after Abraham Icek
Tuschinski, who was Amsterdam's
most illustrious cinematic
entrepreneur. Built in 1921 as
a 'world theatre palace', the
decor is an arresting clash of
rococo, art deco and Jugendstil,
which can make it hard to keep
your eyes on the silver screen.
Glittering premières take place
to road-blocking effect. If you're
more 'in the red' than red carpet-
ready, check out the morning
screenings.

Taboo

Reguliersdwarsstraat 45 (775
3963, www.taboobar.nl). Tram 1,
2, 4, 5, 9, 14, 16. Open 5pm-3am
Mon-Thur; 5pm-4am Fri;
4pm-4am Sat; 4pm-3am Sun.
Hours vary during winter. Map p109
J11 ⑭ *Gay club*

In some ways, it's just another
gay bar – it plays Cher and is
festooned in rainbows – but what
the place lacks in mould-breaking
sparkle, it makes up for in decent
prices and a double happy hour
(6-7pm, 1-2am).

Pathé Tuschinski

Jordaan
& the West

The Jordaan emerged when the city was extended in the 17th century. It was originally designated as an area for the working classes and industrial enterprises, and it also provided a haven for victims of religious persecution, such as the Jews and Huguenots. Despite such proletarian origins, its properties are now highly desirable.

The Jordaan has no major sights; it's a place in which you stumble across things. The area north of the shopping-dense Rozengracht, the Jordaan's approximate mid-point, is picturesque, whereas the area to the south is more commercial.

Between scenic coffee (or beer) breaks, browse the specialist shops and galleries up adorable side streets.

❤ Shortlist

Must-see sights
Lose yourself in the picture-perfect area north of Rozengracht (p118).

Sweet treat
The best apple pie in town at Winkel 43 (p122).

Quiet drink
Old-fashioned boozers Café Nol (p122) and Papeneiland (p122).

Best bargains
Haggle at Noordermarkt (p125) every Monday morning.

Cultural fix
Creative complex Westergasfabriek (p123) fulfils all cultural and culinary needs.

Big night out
Have a laugh at Boom Chicago (p126), nod your head sedately at North Sea Jazz Club (p126) or dance for 24 hours straight at EDM club De School (p126).

Escape the buzz
Explore the area's hidden *hofje* courtyards (p118).

You'll find many markets nearby: Monday morning's Noordermarkt and Saturday's foodie Boerenmarkt take place around the **Noorderkerk**, the city's first Calvinist church, built in 1623. Nearby lies the Westermarkt, and another general market fills Lindengracht on Saturdays. Between Brouwersgracht and Westelijk Eilanden, quirky shops can be found on Haarlemmerstraat and its westerly extension Haarlemmerdijk, where you'll see Haarlemmerpoort city gate, built in 1840.

Northwest of the Jordaan, the **Westerpark** has been reinvigorated by the conversion of an old gasworks into cultural hotspot **Westergasfabriek**, whose clubs, restaurants and performance venues have breathed creative energy into the area. The rest of the Westerpark area is a lively mix of shops and restaurants.

➜ Getting around

Public transport through the Jordaan itself is limited due to the narrow streets. The area is best accessed on foot from the Rozengracht, which is reached via tram 13, 14, 17 or bus 753. Get to Westerpark via tram 10 or bus 21 from Centraal.

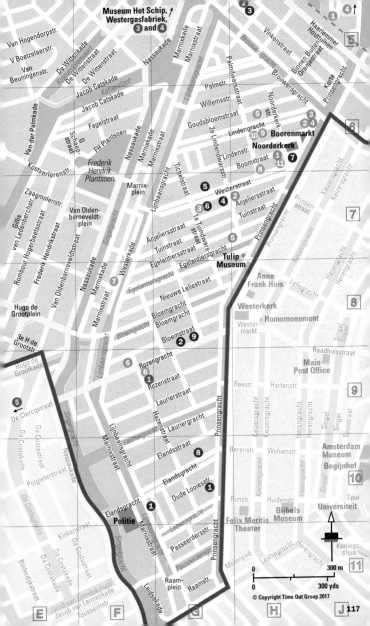

💙 Stroll through the Jordaan

True to form as an artistic neighbourhood, the Jordaan is hailed as one of the most charming and romantic parts of the city. Whether it's the flowers in window boxes, the intriguing street art, the seemingly infinite number of brown bars or the colourful history, the area lures both locals and curious tourists to its enticing streets all year round.

For a walk that takes in a selection of interesting local landmarks, shops and cafés, as well as the most scenic streets and canals, start at **Bloemgracht** and follow what is arguably the most beautiful canal in the Jordaan. Take in its varied façades and well-maintained canal houses. The three houses that make up nos.87-91 (on the south side of the canal) date back to 1642 and are an excellent example of 17th-century Amsterdam architecture. They are known as **De Drie Hendricken** (the Three Hendricken) because of their three gable stones depicting a city-dweller, farmer and sailor.

Cross the canal at Tweede Leliedwarsstraat, heading north for some full-on Amsterdam weirdness at **Electric Ladyland** (Tweede Leliedwarsstraat 5, 420 3776, www.electric-lady-land. com). It's the first museum in the world dedicated to the art, science and history of fluorescent colours. Just round the corner at nos.107-145 Egelantiersgracht, there's the altogether more peaceful **Sint-Andrieshof**, a good example of the Jordaan's secluded residential courtyards, known in Dutch as *hofjes*. Originally built by charitable patrons during the Middle Ages for elderly

women and the vulnerable, these almshouses are now desirable spots to live. Push hard on the door to open and take a seat on one of the benches to absorb the silence away from the bustle outside.

Continue east up Egelantiersgracht as far as the picturesque Tweede Egelantiersdwarsstraat bridge. Cross and continue up the canal on the opposite side until you reach **'t Smalle** (*see p124*). Set on a small canal, it's where Peter Hoppe (of Hoppe & Jenever, the world's first makers of gin) founded his distillery in 1780. It's so charming that the Japanese have built an exact replica of 't Smalle in Nagasaki's Holland Village. Further on you'll find an unassuming red brick building which houses **Claes Claesz Hofje** (Egelantiersdwarsstraat 1-5). The complex, which covers a large part of the block, hides four charming

Noorderkerk

courtyards behind its walls. The first garden has a fountain with a lion's head. These courtyards date to 1626 and are always open to the public.

Carry on past pretty boutiques, cosy cafés and quirky galleries, including **KochxBos** (*see p124*), taking a right on to Westerstraat. For an energy boost stop off at **Winkel 43** (*see p122*) – it's famous for its apple pie, which is reportedly the best in town. This should set you up to explore **Noorderkerk** (North Church), opposite. The Protestant church was built in 1623 and its plain exterior matches the traditionally working-class Jordaan parishioners. Outside the main entrance there's a sculpture of three figures bound together with the inscription '*Eenheid de sterkste keten*' ('the strongest chains are those of unity'). The statue commemorates the bloody Jordaan riots of 1934 against government austerity measures. On the east exterior wall of the church there's a plaque commemorating the February 1941 labour strikes, protesting the deportation of Jews by the occupying Nazis. Every Saturday the church square (**Noordermarkt**) hosts Boerenmarkt (*see p125*), the largest market of organic produce in Amsterdam, and on Monday there's a wonderful flea market (*see p125*).

A ten-minute stroll down Prinsengracht will take you back to where you started on Bloemgracht. If you're curious about the Dutch national symbol, stop in en route at the **Tulip Museum** (Prinsengracht 116, 421 0095, www. amsterdamtulipmuseum.com). It tells the fascinating story of tulip mania, which gripped the city in the 17th-century.

Egelantiersgracht

Sights & museums

Museum Het Schip
Oostzaanstraat 45 (686 8595, www.hetschip.nl). Bus 22. **Open** *11am-5pm Tue-Sun. Guided tours every hr, but only 3pm tour is guaranteed in English.* **Admission** *€12.50; €7.50 reductions; free under-12s, Iamsterdam, MK. No cards.* **Map** *p117 G3.*

Just north of Westerpark, Spaarndammer-plantsoen features three monumental public housing blocks designed by Michel de Klerk, the most expressionist of which is known as Het Schip (The Ship). It's one of the finest examples of the Amsterdam School architectural movement and a must-see for architecture students. The interior is an experience to behold, and exhibitions investigate the importance of public housing.

Restaurants & cafés

't Blaauwhooft €€
Hendrik Jonker Plein 1 (623 8721, www.blaauwhooft.nl). Tram 3 or bus 18, 21, 22. **Open** *3pm-1am Mon-Thur, Sun; 3pm-2am Fri, Sat. Kitchen 6-10pm daily.* **Map** *p117 J5* ❶ *Dutch*

Boasting a large outdoor terrace, the Bickerseiland's picturesque Blaauwhooft has been luring locals and tourists for years. On the menu you'll find traditional Dutch pub favourites, including cheese fondue and mussels

Bordewijk €€€
Noordermarkt 7 (624 3899, www.bordewijk.nl). Tram 3, 10 or bus 18, 21, 22. **Open** *6.30-10.30pm Tue-Sat.* **Map** *p117 H6* ❷ *French*

Come here to sample some of the city's finest original food and palate-tingling wines in a stylish interior. The service and atmosphere are both relaxed, and the kitchen is very reliable.

Comestibles Kinders €
Westerstraat 189 (622 7983). Tram 3, 10 or bus 18, 21. **Open** *7am-5pm Mon-Sat; 9am-4pm Sun.* **Map** *p117 G7* ❸ *Sandwiches*

The best sandwich shop in the Jordaan? Decide over a *bolgeri* with chicken fillet, bacon, pesto, lettuce, mayo and some secret herbs for less than a fiver. There's also a tempting spread of other options.

De Gouden Reael €€
Zandhoek 14 (623 3883, www.goudenreael.nl). Bus 48. **Open** *4pm-1am daily.* **Map** *p117 J5* ❹ *Dutch/Global*

If you're in the market for a wide variety of flavour, De Gouden Reael won't disappoint. Guests can choose from dozens of sharing plates, which range from sherry rib-eye to hazelnut mackerel, for just €9 a pop. The wine menu is just as impressive.

Gs Really Nice Place €€
Goudsbloemstraat 91 (www.reallyniceplace.com). Tram 3, 10. **Open** *10am-4pm Fri-Sun.* **Map** *p117 H6* ❺ *Café*

Resembling a Hipstamatic version of a 'brown café' (all letterpress fonts and vintage crockery), Gs serves a first-rate brunch and hosts quirky pop-up events. It also happens to mix a cracking Bloody Mary. Gs also runs a brunch boat, for breakfast with a canal-side view.

Pesca €€
Rozengracht 133 (334 5136, www.pesca-amsterdam.nl). Tram 13, 14, 17. **Open** *6pm-midnight Tue-Sun.* **Map** *p117 F9* ❻ *Seafood*

Pesca – 'Theatre of Fish' – offers a unique concept for seafood lovers. The restaurant is set up like a fancy fish market. As you enter, you're greeted by a host who will offer a glass of champagne while you peruse the fresh catch – including mussels, cod, scallops and octopus. Once you've chosen, you progress

Museum Het Schip

to the next stage of the restaurant where you tell a different staff member what you'd like to drink and order your sides. Finally, you arrive in the eating hall. The service is fast, the music is loud and the atmosphere is buzzing.

Semhar €€
Marnixstraat 259-261 (638 1634, www.semhar.nl). Tram 10. **Open** *4-10pm Tue-Sun. Main courses €16-€23.* **Map** *p117 F8* ⑦ *Ethiopian*
A great spot to sample the spicy, vegetarian-friendly food of Ethiopia, including *injera* (a type of sourdough pancake), best accompanied by a beer.

SLA €
Westerstraat 34 (370 2733, www. ilovesla.com). Tram 3, 10. **Open** *11am-9pm daily.* **No cash.** **Map** *p117 H6* ⑧ *Salads*
'Sla' means salad. And, indeed, they are organic health freaks here – but in a relaxed and tasty way. Try one of the house 'favourites' (grilled organic chicken with cauliflower, broccoli and red quinoa, perhaps) or create your own personalised salad. To maintain balance, forgo the juices and opt for a locally produced beer from Brouwerij 't IJ.

Toscanini €€€
Lindengracht 75 (623 2813, www. restauranttoscanini.nl). Tram 3, 10. **Open** *3pm-12.30am Mon-Sat; Kitchen 6-10.30pm.* **Map** *p117 H6* ⑨ *Italian*
The food at this popular spot is prepared in an open kitchen. Expect the likes of Sardinian sheep's cheese with chestnut honey and black pepper, or beef tenderloin with rosemary and *lardo di colonnata*. Book in advance to ensure a table. If you don't want to make an evening of it, or are looking for something cheaper, nearby **Capri** (Lindengracht 63, 624 4940) has fine pizza.

Vlaming €€
Lindengracht 95 (622 2716, www. eetcafevlaming.nl). Tram 3, 10. **Open** *6-10pm Tue-Sat.* **Map** *p117 H6* ⑩ *Dutch/Global*
Whether it's for the North Sea-size burgers or Asian-inspired tuna steaks, regulars love this cosy 'eating café' in the heart of the Jordaan. Its second outlet is roomier, more brasserie-like and open seven days a week, but its menu lacks the burger. Book ahead.

♥ Winkel 43 €€

Noordermarkt 43 (623 0223, www. winkel43.nl). Tram 3, 10 or bus 18, 21, 22. **Open** *7am-1am Mon; 8am-1am Tues-Thur; 8am-3am Fri; 7am-3am Sat; 10am-1am Sun.* **Map** *p117 H6* ⑪ *Dutch*

Hailed for having the best apple pie in all of Amsterdam – quite a claim to fame – Winkel 43 is worth a visit. Nestled near the city's scenic Brouwersgracht, look for the green and white shutters and you won't miss it. It also serves other food, including quiche and a delicious brioche burger, but leave room for the famous apple pie. It lives up to the hype.

Bars

Café Hegeraad

Noordermarkt 34 (624 5565). Tram 3, 10 or bus 18, 21. **Open** *8am-1am Mon-Thur; 8am-3am Fri, Sat; 11am-1am Sun.* **No cards.** **Map** *p117 H6* ①

The opposite – geographically as well as figuratively – of minimalist **Proust** (*see p122*) and its neighbour **Finch**, this gabled building with leaded windows has probably been a café for as long as the Noorderkerk church opposite has been standing. Be careful not to spill your drink on the carpeted tables.

In the know
City farm

Just a few minutes by bicycle from Westergasfabriek, you'll come across a friendly neighbourhood farm in the middle of a sheep field. The volunteer-run **Buurtboerderij Ons Genoegen** (Spaarndammerdijk 319, 337 6820, www.buurtboerderij.nl) has a lovely café and organises assorted events throughout the year. Perfect for when the big bad city just gets too much.

♥ Café Nol

Westerstraat 109 (624 5380, cafenol-amsterdam.nl). Tram 3, 10 or bus 18, 21. **Open** *9pm-3am Wed, Thur, Sun; 9pm-4am Fri, Sat.* **Map** *p117 H7* ②

At a glance, it looks like another of the brown bars the Jordaan is known for. But by night, Café Nol transforms into the neon-lit site of Dutch folk sing-alongs for locals and tourists alike. Self-proclaimed as the 'most famous café in the Jordaan', its red shuttered doors hold 50 years of stories, which the older patrons will be happy to share with you after a beer or two.

♥ Papeneiland

Prinsengracht 2 (624 1989, www. papeneiland.nl). Tram 3, 10 or bus 18, 21, 22. **Open** *10am-1am Mon-Thur, Sun; 10am-3am Fri, Sat.* **Map** *p117 J6* ③

This Delft-tiled bar is a wonderful spot for a drink and a chinwag. A definite talking point is the café's fascinating history: apparently, a tunnel runs under the canal, which, when Catholicism was outlawed in the 17th century, secretly delivered worshippers to their church opposite. It certainly explains the bar's name: Pope's Island.

Proust

Noordermarkt 4 (623 9145, www. proust.nl). Tram 3, 10 or bus 18, 21, 22. **Open** *9am-11pm Mon; 11am-1am Tue-Thur, 11am-3am Fri; 9am-3am Sat; 11am-1am Sun.* **Map** *p117 J6* ④

Still trendy after all these years, and great for a market pit stop or to kickstart a bar crawl. The interior is pared down in style – as are the punters. If it's full, try **Finch** next door; on warm days, both bars' terraces merge into one convivial whole to create an atmosphere that is pure Amsterdam.

❤ Westergasfabriek

*Pazzanistraat 37 (586 0710, www.
wester gasfabriek.nl). Tram 10 or
Bus 21. **Open** daily, hours vary.
Admission Free, unless ticketed
event.*

Lying west of the Jordaan within
the Westerpark is a cultural hub
for film, theatre, music and art.
Whether you've got the itch to
wash down some *bitterballen* with
a craft beer, immerse yourself
in the latest art exhibition or
dance to the latest sounds,
chances are Westergasfabriek
is the place to scratch it. But
this local hotspot wasn't always
thriving with the creativity it
effortlessly exudes today. From
1885 to 1967, the Westergasfabriek
(which translates to Western
Gasworks) pumped coal gas into
the homes of Amsterdam.

The heavily polluted site
was left largely untouched for
decades until the early 1990s,
when creative and cultural
pioneers used the space for
temporary showcases.

In 2002, the site was
redeveloped with an entirely
new kind of energy. The former
factory now serves as office spaces
for creative entrepreneurs, and
various high-profile events and
art exhibits are held here, such
as **Unseen Amsterdam**. There
are also excellent cafés, bars and
restaurants on site, including
WestergasTerras (684 8496, www.
westergasterras.nl), microbrewery
and bar **Troost Brewery** (737 1028,
brouwerijtroost.nl/en/westergas-
amsterdam) and seafood
restaurant **Mossel & Gin** (486
5869, www.mosselengin.nl).

't Smalle
*Egelantiersgracht 12 (623 9617, www.t-smalle.nl). Tram 13, 14, 17. **Open** 10am-1am Mon-Thur, Sun; 10am-2am Fri, Sat. **Map** p117 H7* ⑤
This is one of the most scenic terraces on one of the prettiest canals, so it's no surprise that waterside seats are snared early in the day. It's very cute inside too, with gleaming brass fixtures harking back to the heady drinking days of the 18th century, when it was the Hoppe distillery.

Struik
*Rozengracht 160 (06 5260 8837). Tram 10, 13, 14, 17. **Open** 5pm-1am Mon-Thur; 5pm-3am Fri; 3pm-3am Sat; 3pm-1am Sun. **Map** p117 F9* ⑥
A chilled bar for hipsters who like their music cool and their design street. The friendly neighbourhood café vibe is enhanced by budget-priced daily dinner specials. Later on, the DJ kicks in. There's also a larger sister operation up the street, **Brandstof** (Marnixstraat 341, 422 0813, www.bar-brandstof.nl).

Coffeeshops

La Tertulia
*Prinsengracht 312 (www. coffeeshoptertulia.com). Tram 7, 10. **Open** 11am-7pm Tue-Sat. **No cards**. **Map** p117 G10* ①
This mellow mother-and-daughter-run joint is decorated with plenty of plants, a little waterfall and lots of sunlight, which balances harmoniously with the all-bio buds and scrumptious weed brownies. Two floors provide space for relaxation, quiet reading or gazing at the canal. Look for the stoned Van Gogh painted outside.

Shops & services

Antiekcentrum Amsterdam
Elandsgracht 109 (624 9038, www. antiekcentrumamsterdam.nl).

*Tram 7, 10, 17. **Open** 11am-6pm Mon, Wed-Fri; 11am-5pm Sat, Sun. **Map** p117 F10* ① *Antiques*
The 70-plus stalls here deal mainly in antiques, with plenty of collectors' items; you'll find everything from pewter to paintings, and glassware to gold. It's easy to get lost and find yourself standing alone by a stall crammed with antique clocks ticking eerily away.

Les Deux Frères
*Rozengracht 58HS (846 4613, www.lesdeuxfreres.nl). Tram 10, 13, 14, 17. **Open** noon-6.30pm Mon; 10.30am-6.30pm Tue-Fri; 10.30am-6pm Sat; noon-5pm Sun. **Map** p117 G8* ② *Clothing*
The brainchild of brothers Alain and Matthieu, Les Deux Frères is a lifestyle-based clothing store for men, selling a range of quality brands. Designed for males who aren't so fond of shopping, the store also sells coffee. Enough said.

Jutka & Riska
*Haarlemmerdijk 143 (06 2466 8593 mobile, www.jutkaenriska. nl). Bus 18, 22. **Open** 10.30am-7pm Mon-Wed, Fri; 10.30am-9pm Thur; 10am-7pm Sat; noon-6.30pm. **Map** p117 H5* ③ *Fashion*
This kooky store (there are Barbie dolls lurking all over the place) stocks a mix of 'old, new, borrowed and blue' fashion and prides itself on its extensive range of reasonably priced 1950s, 1960s and 1970s frocks. Most cost under €50. There's also second-hand Sonia Rykiel, vintage Yves Saint Laurent blazers and some colourful one-off pieces from the store's Jutka & Riska label.

KochxBos Gallery
*Eerste Anjeliersdwarsstraat 36 (681 4567, www.kochxbos.nl). Tram 13, 14, 17. **Open** 1pm-6pm Wed-Sat. **Map** p117 G7* ④ *Art*

Moooi

Moooi
Westerstraat 187 (528 7760, www. moooi.com). Tram 3, 10. **Open** *10am-6pm Tue-Sat.* **Map** *p117 G7* ⑥ *Homewares*
A former school has been transformed into a Dutch design hub and the studio of design star Marcel Wanders – inventor of the iconic Knotted Chair, and also responsible for the **Andaz Amsterdam** hotel (*see p175*). On the ground floor, step into his stylish store, Moooi, the showroom for his work and the portfolios of other creatives such as Studio Job, Piet Boon and Jurgen Bey. Just don't come here expecting to find any bargains.

♥ Noordermarkt
Noordermarkt (no phone). Tram 3, 10 or bus 18, 21, 22. **Open** *9am-2pm Mon; 9am-4pm Sat.* **No cards.** **Map** *p117 G7* ⑦ *Market*
North of Westermarkt, Noordermarkt is frequented by the serious shopper. The huge stacks of (mainly second-hand) clothes, shoes, jewellery and hats need to be sorted with a grim determination, but there are bargains to be had if you delve deeply. Arrive early or the best stuff will have been nabbed. The organic Boerenmarkt farmers' market is held here on Saturdays.

With a sister studio in New York City, KochxBos Gallery is the first independent low-brow pop-surrealist gallery in Amsterdam. Celebrating contemporary underground art, Kochxbos Gallery has exhibited the up-and-coming likes of Ray Caesar and Meryl Donoghue.

Lena the Fashion Library
Westerstraat 174h (789 1781, www.lena-library.com/vestiging-amsterdam). Tram 3, 10 or bus 18, 21. **Open** *10am-7pm Mon; 11am-7pm Wed, Fri; 11am-8pm Thur; 11am-5pm Sat.* **Map** *p117 G7* ⑤ *Fashion*
Instead of borrowing books, visitors can borrow pre-loved clothing. The founders aim to raise awareness of the negative effects of consumerism – including worker exploitation and textile waste – with their initiative. But there is such a thing as no returns; if you decide you can't part with an item after borrowing it you'll receive a 10 per cent discount on purchase price.

Tenue de Nîmes
Elandsgracht 60 (320 4012, www. tenuedenimes.com). Tram 7, 10. **Open** *noon-7pm Mon; 11am-7pm Tue-Fri; 10am-6pm Sat; noon-6pm Sun.* **Map** *p117 G10* ⑧ *Fashion*
Aptly named after the spiritual home of denim (a French town called Nîmes), this boutique-cum-photography-gallery features bare brick walls adorned with denim-covered beams, antiquated Singer sewing machines and limited-edition Raw Cannondale bicycles. The shop's selection of edgier brands, including Momotaro, Acne and Rag & Bone, is second to none.

Wegewijs

Rozengracht 32 (624 4093). Tram 13, 14, 17. **Open** *8.30am-5.30pm Mon-Fri; 9am-4pm Sat.* **Map** *p117 G8* ❾ *Food & drink*

The Wegewijs family opened this shop more than a century ago. On offer are around 50 foreign and more than 100 domestic varieties of cheese, including *graskaas*, a grassy-tasting cheese that's available in summer. You're allowed to try the Dutch varieties before you buy.

Entertainment

❤ Boom Chicago

Rozentheater, Rozengracht 117 (217 0400, www.boomchicago.nl). Tram 10, 13, 14, 17. **Open** *varies.* **Admission** *varies.* **Map** *p117 F9* ❶ *Comedy*

This American improv troupe is one of Amsterdam's biggest success stories, with alumni including Seth Meyers (*Saturday Night Live*) and Jason Sudekis (*30 Rock*). Several different shows, all in English, run seven nights a week (winter is slightly quieter), featuring a mix of audience-prompted improvisation, rehearsed sketches, full-blown themed shows and guest comedians from around the world – coupled with dinner options.

The Movies

Haarlemmerdijk 161 (638 6016, www.themovies.nl). Tram 3 or bus 18, 21, 22. Screens 4. Tickets €9-€11; €75 10-visit card. **No cards.** **Map** *p117 H5* ❷ *Cinema*

The oldest cinema in Amsterdam to remain in regular use, The Movies has been circulating celluloid since 1912 and still exudes a genteel atmosphere of sophistication.

❤ North Sea Jazz Club

Pazzanistraat 1, Westergasfabriek (722 0980, www.northseajazzclub. com). Tram 10. **Open** *varies.* **Admission** *varies.* **Map** *p117 F5* ❸ *Live music*

Associated with the annual festival North Sea Jazz, this club combines jazz, funk, blues and soul names, big and small, in an intimate setting – with both standing and dinner-club options.

Pacific Parc

Polonceaukade 23, Westergasfabriek (488 7778, www.pacificparc.nl). Tram 10. **Open** *11am-1am Mon-Thur; 11am-3am Fri, Sat; 11am-11pm Sun. Shows usually 11pm/midnight.* **Admission** *free.* **Map** *p117 F5* ❹ *Club*

While its sprawling terrace attracts mums and baby buggies by day, bar-restaurant Pacific Parc attracts the nastier yet compelling aspects of rock 'n' roll by night. Local DJs such as Bone, Mappe, Stuka and Pete Slovenly generally spin from Thursdays to Saturdays, and international badass bands touring the dives of Europe are often asked to complete the line-up.

❤ De School

Dr Jan van Breemenstraat 1 (737 3197, www.deschoolamsterdam.nl). Tram 13. **Open** *varies.* **Admission** *varies.* **Map** *p117 E4* ❺ *Club*

Lovers of the night were gutted when legendary Amsterdam club Trouw closed its doors, but they didn't have to wait long for a replacement. Set on a school campus from the 1960s, De School is the Trouw team's entry into the thriving electronic dance scene. It's one of a growing number of clubs to hold a 24-hour licence, which means some nights go on until 10am. The 500-capacity club is part of a wider cultural centre at the former campus, which also includes a concert venue, restaurant, café and exhibition space. If you're going to make a night of it, make sure you know who is playing – the exceptionally trendy staff on the door are quick to turn away perceived posers.

Museum Quarter, Oud West & Zuid

The heart of the late 19th-century Museum Quarter lies in **Museumplein**, the city's largest square, bordered by the Concertgebouw, Rijksmuseum, Stedelijk Museum and Van Gogh Museum. Museumplein itself is not an authentic Amsterdam square, but it does have plenty of grass, a wading pool, skate ramp and the much-photographed oversized IAmsterdam letters.

As you would expect in such surroundings, the affluence is apparent. Housing comes in the form of elegant 19th-century mansions, and Van Baerlestraat and PC Hooftstraat are as close as Amsterdam gets to Rodeo Drive.

Classic art
Van Gogh Museum (p137) has a lifetime's body of work by the post-Impressionist genius, and the Rijksmuseum (p130) is the nation's unmissable treasure house.

Eclectic shopping
Marqt (p136) for fresh organic food and Mashed Concept Store (p136) for a bit of everything.

Start the day
Have a hangover-busting brunch at Staring at Jacob (p135) or hipster coffee at Lot Sixty One (p133).

Modern art
Contemporary art galore at the Stedelijk Museum (p134) and new kid on the Museumplein block, Moco (p132).

Inspired dining
Indoor food hall with a world of choice at Foodhallen (p133).

Cultural fix
Take in the acoustics at Concertgebouw (p140), one of the world's best concert venues.

Escape the buzz
Take a break from trams and bikes in Vondelpark (p138).

Vondelpark is the city's most central park, and the last few years have witnessed much renovation to stop it from sinking. There are several ponds and lakes, along with play areas and cafés. Vondelpark gets fantastically busy on sunny days and Sundays. Films, plays and public concerts are also staged, with a festival of free open-air performances taking place in the summer.

Stretching out in the shape of a ring beneath Vondelpark is a fairly indeterminate region known as **Nieuw Zuid** (New South), which is bordered to the east by the Amstel and to the west by the 1928 Olympisch Stadion.

To the north of Vondelpark is **Oud West**. Now abuzz with cafés and boutiques, this leafy and lively suburb housed the city's smelly industries and plague victims in the 17th century. In the 19th century it was developed to make way for working-class families and since then has flourished into a charming – and impeccably clean – area.

➡ **Getting around**
Trams 1, 2, 5, 7 and 17 run from Centraal Station through the Museum Quarter and Oud West towards Zuid. Bike paths are established throughout the area.

♥ Rijksmuseum

MUSEUM QUARTER, OUD WEST & ZUID

Museumstraat 1 (674 7000, www. rijksmuseum.nl). Tram 2, 5, 7, 10. **Open** *9am-5pm daily.* **Admission** *€17.50; €8.75 reductions; free under-19s, MK.* **Map** *p129 H13.*

Originally designed by PJH Cuypers and opened in 1885, the nation's 'treasure house' is home to 40 Rembrandt and four Vermeer paintings – and holds up a mirror to Centraal Station, also built by Cuypers. The collection was started when William V began to acquire pieces just for the hell of it, and has been growing ever since. Besides Rembrandt's *The Night Watch* plus Vermeer's *Milkmaid* and *Woman Reading a Letter*, it also has works by the likes of Frans Hals, Jacob de Wit and Ferdinand Bol, as well as a 1917 biplane. There's also a wealth of Asian and decorative arts on display, including 17th-century furniture, intricate silver and porcelain, and 17th- and early 18th-century dolls' houses. All this, plus temporary exhibitions and the museum's freely accessible garden, filled with Dutch Golden Age gateways and architectural fragments.

In the early 21st century, the Rijksmuseum was closed for a decade and €375 million of renovation. It reopened to much fanfare in 2013, and Spanish architect firm Cruz y Ortiz was awarded the prestigious Abe Bonnema Prize for its masterful work, recreating the museum's original clear layout. Minimal alternations were made to the building itself, but the redesign transformed the 19th-century building into the bright, spacious and awe-inspiring 21st-century museum it is today. British historian Simon Schama called the design 'an inauguration of a curatorial revolution'. He said: 'When you see those early Rembrandts or the great mannerist *Massacre of the Innocents* of Cornelis van Haarlem with its ballet of twisting rumps, you will also encounter, as would those who would first have seen them, the silver, weapons and cabinets that were the furniture of the culture that made those pictures possible.'

It's easy to be completely consumed by a museum of this stature, and it's certainly a worthy way to spend the best part of a day. The museum is laid out over

The Milkmaid (Johannes Vermeer, 1658)

four floors numbered from zero to three, but the collections aren't laid out chronologically. If you want to take a walk through the ages, start in the basement (where the main entrance is) for the Middle Ages and the Renaissance, then head up to the 17th-century rooms on Floor 2. Eighteenth- and 19th-century artefacts (plus a few Van Goghs) are housed back down on Floor 1, and there is a limited 20th-century collection on Floor 3. However, if you can't spare a full day to devour the museum's historical delights, head straight to Floor 2, where you'll find the finest works of the Dutch Golden Age on show in the Gallery of Honour, culminating with Rembrandt's *The Night Watch* (officially titled *Militia Company of District II under the Command of Captain Frans Banninck Cocq*; 1642). The Asia Pavilion, a new addition courtesy of Cruz y Ortiz, is separate to the main museum and accessed from the entrance foyer. If you want to avoid the crowds, visit between Monday and Thursday, either right on opening or after 3pm.

There is also a vaulted cycle passage that goes through the museum, so keep an eye out for passing cyclists while you're standing in line. Don't miss the museum's excellent website; book tickets online to avoid the queues.

▶ *Visit the Rembrandthuis to see the world's largest collection of Rembrandt's sketches; see p146.*

Saul and the Witch of Endor (Jacob Cornelisz van Oostsanen, 1526)

The Night Watch (Rembrandt van Rijn, 1642)

Sights & museums

CoBrA Museum of Modern Art

Sandbergplein 1 (547 5050, www.cobra-museum.nl). Tram 5 or Metro 51 or bus 754. **Open** *11am-5pm Tue-Sun.* **Admission** *€12; €7.50 reductions; free under-6s, Iamsterdam, MK. No cards (except shop). Off map.*

An acronym for Copenhagen, Brussels and Amsterdam – the cities from which the key artists of the movement hailed – the marvellous CoBrA Museum of Modern Art includes masterpieces by the avant-garde artists of the original CoBrA movement, as well as work by contemporary artists. The CoBrA artists created a style unimpeded by academic traditions, marked by vibrant colours and created with a sense of spontaneity. The museum itself is a beautiful airy space with an abundance of natural light and a view over a swan-dotted canal bordered by weeping willows. Its permanent collection contains about 300 paintings, sculptures and works on paper, as well as archived documents from the CoBrA era.

♥ Moco Museum

Honthorststraat 20 (370 1997, www. mocomuseum.com). Tram 2, 5. **Open** *10am-6pm daily.* **Admission** *€12.50; €7.50 under-16s. Iamsterdam, MK.* **Map** *p129 G14.*

Once you've had your fill of Old Masters, try some modern masterpieces from the 'rockstars of modern art' instead. The Modern Contemporary (Moco) Museum Amsterdam is located on the Museumplein at Villa Alsberg, a townhouse designed in 1904 by Eduard Cuypers, cousin of PJH Cuypers, architect of the nearby Rijksmuseum. Moco opened its doors in April 2016 with acclaimed Warhol and Banksy exhibitions – many of the pieces borrowed from private collections – and followed with shows by Os Gemeos, KAWS and Maya Hayuk.

Restaurants & cafés

Bagels & Beans €
Van Baerlestraat 40 (675 7050, www.bagelsbeans.nl). Tram 2, 3, 5, 12. **Open** *8am-5.30pm Mon-Fri; 8.30am-5.30pm Sat, Sun.* **Map** *p129 F14* ① *Café*

An Amsterdam success story, this branch of B&B has a wonderfully peaceful back patio. It's perfect for an economical breakfast, lunch or snack; sun-dried tomatoes are employed with particular skill, elevating the humble sandwich to the status of something far more sublime.

❤ Foodhallen €€
Bellamyplein 51 (2926 5037, www. foodhallen.nl). Tram 7, 17. **Open** *11am-11.30pm Mon-Thur, Fri, Sun; 11am-1am Sat.* **Map** *p129 E12* ② *Global*

Located in the tram-depot-turned-cultural complex De Hallen, the Food Hallen is an indoor food market with something to satisfy every hankering. Serving a delicious array of imported beers, the Foodhallen is often full of locals enjoying a meal or drink with friends. On a cold winter's night you can't go past the wood-fired pizzas and if you're visiting in the warmer months the Vietnamese summer rolls never disappoint. It gets busy at peak times, so if you're with a big group head there earlier to nab a seat.

Le Garage €€€€
Ruysdaelstraat 54-56 (679 7176, www.restaurantlegarage.nl). Tram 3, 5, 12, 16, 24. **Open** *noon-2pm, 6-11pm Mon-Fri; 6-11pm Sat, Sun.* **Map** *p129 G16* ③ *French*

Don't your glad rags to blend in at this fashionable brasserie, which is great for emptying your wallet while you watch a selection of ageing Dutch glitterati do exactly the same. The authentic French regional cuisine – and 'worldly' versions thereof – is pretty good.

Hap Hmm €
1e Helmerstraat 33 (618 1884, www. hap-hmm.nl). Tram 1, 7, 10. **Open** *5-9.15pm Mon-Fri.* **No cards.** **Map** *p129 F12* ④ *Dutch*

Hungry but hard up? You need some of the Dutch grandma cooking served in this canteen with a living-room feel. 'Yummy Bite', as the name translates, will happily fill your empty insides with meat and potatoes for not much more than €7.

❤ Lot Sixty One €€
Kinkerstraat 112 (1605 4227, lotsixtyonecoffee.com). Tram 17. **Open** *8am-6pm Mon-Fri; 9am-6pm Sat; 10am-6pm Sun.* **Map** *p129 D11* ⑤ *Café*

It's a coffee snob's paradise and one of the biggest players in the local caffeine scene, supplying beans to cafés and restaurants across Amsterdam. The tiny café is often overflowing with coffee-lovers, but it's worth the wait: coffee here is the best in the city.

Pastis €€€
1e Constantijn Huygensstraat 15 (616 6166, www.pastisamsterdam. nl). Tram 1, 3, 12. **Open** *5pm-1am Mon-Thur; 5pm-2am Fri; 3pm-2am Sat; 3pm-1am Sun.* **Map** *p129 E12* ⑥ *Brasserie*

This Pastis may not be in New York's meatpacking district, but the neighbourhood favourite sure packs a punch when it comes to brasserie classics, from caesar salad to crème brûlée. Generous opening hours make it the perfect choice for a very easy Sunday afternoon.

Riaz €
Bilderdijkstraat 193 (683 6453, www.riaz.nl). Tram 3, 7, 12, 17. **Open** *1pm-9pm Mon-Fri; 2-9pm Sun.* **No cards.** **Map** *p129 E11* ⑦ *Surinamese*

A household name in these parts, Riaz is one of Amsterdam's finest Surinamese restaurants. Since 1981,

♥ Stedelijk Museum

Museumplein 10 (573 2911, www. stedelijk.nl). Tram 2, 5, 12. **Open** *10am-6pm Mon-Thur, Sat, Sun; 10am-10pm Fri.* **Admission** *€15; €7.50 reductions; free under-18s, Iamsterdam, MK. Temporary exhibitions vary. No cards (except shop).* **Map** *p129 G14.*

With a world-class, diverse collection, the Stedelijk Museum holds its own on the international modern art stage. Pre-war highlights include works by Cézanne, Picasso, Matisse and Chagall, plus a collection of paintings and drawings by the Russian constructivist Kasimir Malevich. Among post-1945 artists in the collection are minimalists Donald Judd, Barnett Newman and Frank Stella, pop artists Roy Lichtenstein, Sigmar Polke and Andy Warhol, abstract expressionists Karel Appel and Willem De Kooning, and conceptual artists Jan Dibbets, Jeff Koons and Bruce Nauman. You'll also find work by local heroes such as video artist Aernout Mik and painter Marlene Dumas. And there is also an excellent display of 2,000 design objects – including a complete bedroom by Gerrit Rietveld from 1926 – which provide evidence of why the Netherlands remains at the vanguard internationally in this field. On the ground floor, you'll find a historic display of visual art and design dating back to 1850, while the top floor boasts an awe-inspiring permanent collection spanning Warhol and more recent acquisitions by Flavin and Dumas.

After roaming homeless for years, the Stedelijk Museum returned to its revamped building in 2012 following an eight-year wait. The extension, aptly dubbed the 'bathtub' by locals, is made of shiny composite fibre more commonly used for the hulls of yachts. Architect Benthem Crowel created the extension, which hulks over the rather ho-hum original 1895 building. It also provides a very grand entrance that faces Museumplein square instead of

Wall Drawing #1084 (Sol LeWitt, 2003)

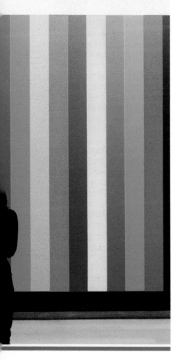

the street. Inside, the contrasts come together in presenting the best of the Stedelijk's collection of 90,000 objects.

Peak times are weekends and holiday periods, when you can wait up to an hour in line. If you're no good with crowds, a Monday or Friday night visit is always a good option. If you decide on the latter and want to make a date of it, **Restaurant Stedelijk** provides a delicious three-course meal; call 573 2651 for reservations.

the chefs have been cooking their exclusive and authentic recipes. You have to taste it to believe it.

Ron Gastrobar €€
Sophialaan 55 (496 1943, www. rongastrobar.nl). Tram 2. **Open** *noon-2.30pm every day; 5.30-10.20pm Mon-Sun; 5-10.30pm Sun.* **Map** *p129 A16* ❽ *Modern Dutch*
Ron Gastrobar is named after local entrepreneurial celebrity chef Ron Blaauw, who put his two Michelin stars on the line by coming up with a simpler, more affordable menu of 25 no-nonsense back-to-basics mains costing €15 each.

♥ Staring at Jacob €€
Jacob van Lennepkade 215 (223 7498, www.staringatjacob.nl). Tram 1. **Open** *11am-5pm Mon, Thur, Fri; 10am-5pm Sat, Sun.* **Map** *p129 B13* ❾ *American*
This American-inspired café is the perfect place to go for hearty hangover food. With fried chicken waffles, fluffy butternut pancakes and BLTs to make you salivate, there's also a mean Bloody Mary on the menu for hair of the dog.

Bars

't Blauwe Theehuis
Vondelpark 5 (662 0254, www. blauwetheehuis.nl). Tram 1, 2, 3, 5, 12. **Open** *9am-6pm Mon-Thur; 9am-8pm Fri-Sun (hours extended on sunny weekends).* **Map** *p129 E14* ❶
One of the few local landmarks that allows you to nestle inside with a beer, HAJ Baanders' extraordinary 1930s teahouse – a sort of UFO/hat hybrid in the middle of Vondelpark – is a choice spot for fair-weather drinking, with its huge terrace. In summer, there are DJs and barbecues, although it's a romantic spot for dinner and drinks all year round.

Café Welling

Jan Willem Brouwerstraat 32 (662 0155, www.cafewelling.nl). Tram 2, 3, 5, 12. **Open** *4pm-1am Mon-Sat, 4pm-midnight Sun.* **Map** *p129 F15* ❷

Just behind the Concertgebouw, brownish Welling offers plenty of choice in the beer department – plus excellent, locally produced *jenever*. The welcoming atmosphere is in contrast to many of the other overpriced, posh spots near here. Be charmed by the regulars, who often come in carrying their instruments.

Café Wildschut

Roelof Hartplein 1-3 (676 8220, www.cafewildschut.nl). Tram 3, 5, 12, 24. **Open** *9am-midnight Mon; 9am-1am Tue-Thur; 9am-2am Fri, 10am-2am Sat; 10am-midnight Sun.* **Map** *p129 G15* ❸

A stunning example of Amsterdam School architecture, this elegant semi-circular place puts the 'grand' into grand café and drips with nouveau detail. Drink and food choices mirror the upmarket surroundings, as do the clientele, which include flush locals, loud yuppies and art-weary tourists in need of refuelling.

Gollem's Proeflokaal

Overtoom 160-162 (612 9444, www. cafegollem.nl). Tram 1, 3, 12. **Open** *1pm-1am Mon-Thur; noon-3am Fri, Sat; noon-1am Sun.* **No cards.** **Map** *p129 E13* ❹

An outstanding place to get sozzled, this dark and cosy Belgian beer specialist offers more than 150 bottled brews – including 42 abbey beers and 14 trappist – and 21 on tap, from easy-drinkers to demonic head-pounders such as Delirium Tremens. There's also a pubby food menu.

Kaasplank

Shops & services

♥ Marqt

Overtoom 21 (820 8292, www. marqt.com). Tram 1, 2, 3, 5, 7, 12. **Open** *9am-9pm daily.* **No cash.** **Map** *p129 F12* ❶ *Food & drink*

Amsterdam's newest organics market focuses on fresh produce, meat and fish sourced from local and regional farmers and independent producers. It also sells great fresh bread from Brood bakery and pizzas from De Pizza Bakker. Products are predominately fair trade too.

♥ Mashed Concept Store

Jan Pieter Heijestraat 168 (64028 7335, www.mashed-concept-store. com). Tram 1. **Open** *noon-6pm Mon; 11am-6pm Tue-Thur; 10am-6pm Fri; 10am-5pm Sat; noon-5pm Sun.* **Map** *p129 C13* ❷ *Gifts*

This charming concept store looks like something you would see on Pinterest. Exposed lights dangle from an all-white ceiling to illuminate the quirky and unique offering of interiors and clothing. A great place for gifts or for an authentic reminder of your trip.

♥ Van Gogh Museum

*Paulus Potterstraat 7 (570 5200, www.vangoghmuseum.nl). Tram 2, 3, 5, 12. **Open** 9am-5pm Mon-Thur, Sat, Sun; 9am-10pm Fri. **Admission** €17; free under-18s, Iamsterdam, MK. Temporary exhibitions vary. **Map** p129 G14.*

The Van Gogh Museum lures art enthusiasts, historians and curious tourists year-round, and is the second most visited museum in the Netherlands with good reason. As well as the bright colours of his palette, Vincent van Gogh is best known for his productivity, and this is reflected in the sheer volume of work permanently exhibited here. With more than 200 paintings, 500 drawings and 700 hand-written letters, the museum houses the world's largest collection of works by the artist.

The Van Gogh Museum first opened in Museumplein in 1973, and has since evolved to become a cutting-edge exhibition space consisting of two buildings: the main Rietveld Building and the Kurokawa Wing – a new glass and steel entrance hall opened in 2015 to connect the two. The main building exhibits everything Van Gogh, with each section dedicated to a different era. To follow the timeline of his tragic life, start at the bottom then make your way up to the third floor. The second floor provides background information about Van Gogh's life, family and friends, including the original letters he wrote to his brother and other relatives. The exhibition wing serves to add perspective to Van Gogh's artistic efforts, with examples of Japanese prints and work by the likes of Manet, Monet and Toulouse-Lautrec. Temporary exhibitions focusing on Van Gogh's contemporaries and his influence on other artists are assembled from both the museum's own extensive archives and private collections.

▶ *To avoid the queues book online, or try visiting either between 9am and 11am or late afternoon. A walk through the museum will only take an hour or two. It's worth noting that Friday evenings often feature lectures, concerts and films.*

MUSEUM QUARTER, OUD WEST & ZUID

💙 Vondelpark

Vondelpark is named after the city's best-known poet, Joost van den Vondel, whose controversial play *Lucifer* caused the religious powers of the 17th century to crack down hard on those who engaged in what was termed 'notorious living'. This is the most central of the city's major parks. Its creation was inspired by the redevelopment of the Plantage, which, until the 19th century, had provided green surroundings for the leisurely walks of the rich. The original ten acres opened in 1865 and were designed in the 'English style' by Jan David Zocher, with the emphasis on natural landscaping. The park has actually sunk some two to three metres since it was first built – some larger trees are either 'floating' on blocks of styrofoam or reinforced with underground poles.

There are several ponds and lakes in the park plus a number of play areas and cafés, including **'t Blauwe Theehuis** (*see p135*) and the **Groot Melkhuis** (612 9674, www.grootmelkhuis.nl), a chalet-style café by the water with a terrace and kids' playground.

Keep your eye out for a huge Picasso sculpture in the middle of the park, and for the wild parakeets that were accidentally released in 1976 and have spread across the city. Round the corner – and providing a unique place for coffee – is the **Hollandsche Manege** (Vondelstraat 140, 618 0942, www.dehollandschemanege. nl), a wooden version of the Spanish Riding School in Vienna. It has been teaching people to ride for well over 100 years.

Vondelpark gets insanely busy on sunny days and Sundays, when bongos abound, dope is toked and football games take up any space that happens to be left over. Hundreds of avid runners and cyclists use it for their daily dose of exercise. The **Vondelpark Openluchttheater** (www.openluchttheater.nl), a long-running programme of free open-air films, plays and concerts takes place throughout the summer.

The south-western end of the park runs along Amstelveenseweg, a varying culinary strip very much worth cruising. Head to **Ron Gastrobar** (*see p135*), but if that's busy, there are a lot of other options too.

For decades, Vondelpark, and especially its rose garden, has also been a notorious midnight

meet-up spot for gay men looking for some frisky risk-taking, but it wasn't until 2008 that the Amsterdam district council, in a display of typical Dutch pragmatism, proclaimed a new set of rules announcing the official 'toleration' of public sex in the park. 'As long as other people in the park don't feel disturbed, then there is no problem with it,' said one politician at the time. According to the 'house rules', enjoying a garden romp is only permitted after dark, and condoms must be cleared away to keep the surrounds tidy. Police officers cannot interrupt the fun unless participants are causing a public nuisance, such as broadcasting their enjoyment too noisily or appearing too close to a public path.

Filmhallen

Hannie Dankbaarpassage 12 (820 8122, www.filmhallen.nl). Tram 3, 17. Screens 9. Tickets €7.50-€11. **No cards.** *Map p129 D11* ❶ *Cinema*
Set inside the train-depot-turned-trendy-spot De Hallen, Filmhallen is the sister to Amsterdam's oldest cinema, The Movies (*see p126*) and one of the largest cinemas in the city. It shows an eclectic mix of movies, from Hollywood blockbusters to quirky arthouse films. For a real treat, grab some streetfood from nearby Foodhallen beforehand.

OT301

Overtoom 301 (412 2954, www. ot301.nl). Tram 1. **Open** *varies.* **Admission** *varies. Map p129 C13* ❷ *Club*
This multipurpose venue offers cheap bottled beer and a wildly varied programme, including Haunted Science drum 'n' bass nights, Matjesdisco ('Mullet Disco') or a savvy selection of bands and DJs from alternative-minded Subbacultcha. Music tends to be on the less commercial side of things. If you don't like the music, OT301 also has a radio station, vegan restaurant and arthouse cinema to keep you entertained.

De Trut

Bilderdijkstraat 165 (www. trutfonds.nl). Tram 3, 7, 12, 17. **Open** *10pm-4am Sun.* **Admission** *varies.* **No cards.** *Map p129 E11* ❸ *Gay club*
If you don't want the weekend to end, head to this alternative gay dance night in a former squat. With all-inclusive drink offers for €20, it's cheap, crowded and fun, and has been running for nearly 40 years. Arrive early, certainly before 11pm, to avoid the queue.

MUSEUM QUARTER, OUD WEST & ZUID

💜 Concertgebouw

Concertgebouwplein 10 (0900 671 8345 premium rate, www. concertgebouw.nl). Tram 2, 3, 5, 12, 16. Box office 1-7pm Mon-Fri; 9am-7pm Sat, Sun. Tickets prices vary. **Map** *p129 G15*

With over 900 events and 700,000 visitors each year, it's safe to say the Concertgebouw has made a mark since its opening in 1888. Occupying prime real estate on Museumplein, alongside the Van Gogh, Stedelijk and Rijks museums, the imperious-looking building has been the epicentre of classical music in the Netherlands for decades. Combining beautiful neoclassical architecture with crystal-clear acoustics, it is a favourite venue of many of the world's top musicians and

has hosted the likes of Gustav Mahler, Richard Strauss, Yehudi Menuhin and Cecilia Bartoli during its illustrious career. Even if you're not a classical music buff, you will still appreciate the surroundings. Designed by architect Adolf Leonard van Gendt, the Concertgebouw is comprised of three halls – the Main Hall, the Recital Hall and the more recent Choir Hall. The unrivalled acoustic properties of the Main Hall make it one of the most revered classical music venues in the world. Tickets are available online and for purchase at the box office via telephone. If you don't have the time (or funds) to treat yourself to a show, be sure to stop by and soak up the sheer grandeur of the building.

Jodenbuurt, Plantage & Oost

Located south-east of the Red Light District and bordered by the IJ harbour to the north, Amsterdam's Jewish quarter is a mix of old and new architectural styles. Crossing the bridge at the end of Sint Antoniesbreestraat leads you to the **Rembrandthuis**, where Rembrandt lived and worked for two decades. Immediately before this, however, are steps to the **Waterlooplein** flea market, dominated by the **Nationale Opera & Ballet**. Also close at hand are the **Joods Historisch Museum** (Jewish Historical Museum) and **Hermitage Amsterdam**.

Stroll down Muiderstraat to discover the largely residential and more verdant **Plantage** area that lies south-east of Mr Visserplein. The attractive Plantage

Old Master
Walk in Rembrandt's footsteps at Rembrandthuis (*p146*), his original place of work.

Living history
Discover the story of the Dutch Resistance in World War II at the Verzetsmuseum (*p147*) and Amsterdam's Jewish past at the Joods Historisch Museum (*p146*).

Walk on the wild side
There's everything from microbes to elephants at Artis Royal Zoo (*p144*).

Cultural fix
Nationale Opera & Ballet (*p150*) is the custom-built home of high culture.

Beer break
Brouwerij 't IJ (*p148*) for beer brewed in the shadow of a windmill.

High- and low-end dining
Enjoy fine French food at La Rive (*p148*) when money is no object or a cone of *friet* from Dappermarkt when it is...

Escape the buzz
Retreat to the peaceful Hortus Botanicus (*p145*), a botanical garden, founded in 1638.

Dusk till dawn
Canvas (*p150*) is a rooftop café during the day, club by night. Fabulous skyline views 24 hours a day.

Middenlaan winds past the **Hortus Botanicus**, near the **Verzetsmuseum** (Museum of Dutch Resistance), and along the edge of **Artis**, the city zoo, towards the **Tropenmuseum**.

Jews began to settle here more than 200 years ago, and the area soon grew with the investment of 19th-century diamond money. The Plantage is still wealthy, with graceful buildings and tree-lined streets, although its charm has sadly faded somewhat.

Further south of Mauritskade is Amsterdam Oost (East), with its green heart **Oosterpark** and multicultural vibe. This area was developed in the late 19th century to provide housing for the city's lower-income families; many immigrants from Morocco, Suriname and Turkey settled in Oost during the 1960s and 1970s, and the low rents lured students and artists to the area in the decades to follow.

200 m
200 yds
© Copyright Time Out Group 2017

Oostenburger-park
Boulevaardpad
Oostenburgergracht

Brouwerij 't IJ

Museum
't Kromhout

Hoogte Kadijk

Overhaalsgang

Wittenburgergracht
Nieuwevaart

Nieuwe Vaart
Hoogte Kadijk
Laagte Dijk
Entrepotdok

Kadijks-plein

Entrepotdok

Rapenburg-plein

Anne Frankstraat

Nieuwe Herengracht

Nieuwe Uilenburgerstr.

Uilenburgerstr.

Gassan
Diamonds

Rembrandthuis

Zuiderkerk
Zandstraat

Oudeschans

Jodenbreestraat

Stadhuis

Nationale
Opera & Ballet

Waterloo-plein
Mozes en
Aäronkerk

Waterloo-plein

Blauw-brug

Amstel

Museum
Willet-Holthuysen

Herengracht

Amstelstr.

Prinsengracht

Keizersgracht

Kerkstraat

Utrechtsedwarsstraat
Utrechtsestr.

143

Verzetsmuseum

Planetarium

Plantage Doklaan

Artis Zoo

Aquarium

Plantage Middenlaan

Plantage Kerklaan

Henri
Polaklaan

Hollandsche
Schouwburg

Plantage Parklaan

Wertheim-park

Hortus
Botanicus

Plantage Muidergracht

Plantage Muidergracht

Westerman-plantsoen

Nieuwe Keizersgracht

Hortusplantsoen

Portuguese
Synagogue

JD Meijer-plein

Joods
Historisch
Museum

Mr Visserplein

Muiderstr.

Markenplein

Vakenburgerstr.

Plantage Badlaan

Weesperstraat

Nieuwe Kerkstraat

Nieuwe Prinsengracht

Amstel

Hermitage
Amsterdam

Magere
Brug

Koninklijk
Theater Carré

Nieuwe Achtergracht

Weesper-plein
Weesperplein

Roetersstr.

Nieuwe Prinsengracht

Nieuwe Achtergracht

Valckenierstraat

Sarphatistraat

Spinozahof

Nieuwe Achtergracht

Nieuwe Roetersstr.

Spinozastr.

Spinozastraat

Tropenmuseum

Oosterpark

Mauritskade

Alexander-plein
Alexanderkade

Kazernestraat

Sarphatistraat

Mauritskade

Singelgracht

Mauritskade

Sajetplein

Singelgracht

Blomberg-plein
Olifants-brug

Sarphatistraat

Plantage Muidergracht

Plantage Middenlaan

Von Zesenstraat

Commelinstraat

Wagenaarstraat

Linnaeusstraat

1e van Swindenstr.

apexstraat

Brouwerij 't IJ

Entrepotdok

Nieuwe Herengracht

Nieuwe Herengracht

Geological Museum at Artis Royal Zoo

Sights & museums

💜 Artis Royal Zoo

Plantage Kerklaan 38-40 (523 3694, www.artis.nl). Tram 9, 14. **Open** *Summer 9am-6pm daily. Winter 9am-5pm daily.* **Admission** *€20.50; €17 reductions; free under-3s. No cards.* **Map** *p143 P11.*
Founded in 1838, Artis was the first zoo in mainland Europe. It was open exclusively to members only until 1851. Today, the zoo is home to more than 750 species of animals, including giraffes, elephants and zebras. It is an active member of the European Endangered Species breeding programme and has close affiliations with the Zoological Museum Amsterdam.

Along with the usual animals, Artis has an indoor 'rainforest' for nocturnal creatures and a 120-year-old aquarium with a simulated canal, complete with eels and bike wrecks. Further attractions include a planetarium, a geological museum and, for kids, a petting zoo and playgrounds.

Hermitage Amsterdam

Amstel 51 (530 7488, www. hermitage.nl). Tram 9, 14 or Metro Waterlooplein. **Open** *10am-5pm daily.* **Admission** *€17.50; €2.50-€15 reductions; free under-11s, Iamsterdam, MK.* **Map** *p143 M11.*
The Amsterdam outpost of St Petersburg's State Hermitage Museum is set in a former 19th-century hospital with a 17th-century courtyard, and has two vast exhibition spaces, a concert hall and a restaurant. The museum mounts two exhibitions a year, borrowing items from the

→ Getting around

Jodenbuurt is centrally located to the east of the Old Centre; it is walking distance from Nieuwmarkt. Trams 9 and 14 run through Jodenbuurt to the Plantage, and trains on the Metro Waterlooplein depart regularly.

three-million-strong collection of its prestigious Russian parent. The Hermitage's riches owe much to the collecting obsession of Peter the Great (1672-1725), who came to Amsterdam to learn shipbuilding and the art of building on waterlogged ground – the latter knowledge he applied to his pet project, St Petersburg. Exhibitions here include Rembrandt, French Impressionists or archaeological discoveries from the Silk Route.

Hollandsche Schouwburg

Plantage Middenlaan 24 (531 0310, www. hollandscheschouwburg.nl). Tram 9, 14 or Metro Waterlooplein. **Open** *11am-5pm daily.* **Admission** *donations accepted (or as part of admission to Joods Historish Museum or Portuguese Synagogue).* **Map** *p143 O11.*

In 1942, this theatre became a main point of assembly for around 80,000 of the city's Jews before they were taken to the transit camp at Westerbork. It is now a monument with a small but impressive exhibition and a memorial hall displaying 6,700 surnames by way of tribute to the 104,000 Dutch Jews who were exterminated.

❤ Hortus Botanicus

Plantage Middenlaan 2A (625 9021, www.dehortus.nl). Tram 9, 14 or Metro 51, 53, 54. **Open** *10am-5pm daily.* **Admission** *€8.50; €1-€5 reductions.* **Map** *p143 O11.*

The Hortus has been a peaceful oasis since 1682, although it was set up more than 50 years earlier when East India Company ships brought back tropical plants and seeds to supply doctors with medicinal herbs (as well as coffee plant cuttings, one specimen of which continued to Brazil to kickstart the South American coffee industry). Highlights include the oldest potted plant in the world, a 300-year-old cycad, in the 1912 palm greenhouse. Other conservatories maintain desert, tropical and subtropical climates, and a butterfly greenhouse sets hearts of all ages aflutter.

Tours are given every Sunday at 2pm. No reservation is required; just keep an eye out for the two guides standing under the large oak tree near the entrance.

Hermitage Amsterdam

Rembrandthuis

💜 Joods Historisch Museum

Nieuwe Amstelstraat 1 (531 0310, www.jhm.nl). Tram 9, 14 or Metro Waterlooplein. **Open** *11am-5pm daily. Closed Jewish New Year & Yom Kippur.* **Admission** *(incl Portuguese Synagogue and Hollandse Schouwburg) €15; €3.75-€7.50 reductions; free under-6s, Iamsterdam, MK.* **Map** *p143 N11.*
Located in the heart of the Jewish quarter, the Jewish Historical Museum is housed in four former synagogues dating back to the 17th and 18th centuries. The museum is packed with religious items, photographs and paintings detailing the history of Jews and Judaism in the Netherlands throughout the centuries. It features both permanent and rotating exhibits.

The museum has received much critical acclaim and attracts thousands of tourists annually. The special children's wing allows youngsters to follow the life of a Jewish family and partake in special activities.

Portuguese Synagogue

Mr Visserplein 3 (531 0380, www. portuguesesynagogue.nl). Tram 9, 14 or Metro Waterlooplein. **Open** *10am-5pm Mon-Thur, Sun; 10am-2pm Fri. Hours may change in different seasons. Closed Yom Kippur.* **Admission** *(incl Joods Historisch Museum and Hollandse Schouwburg) €15; €3.75-€7.50 reductions; free under-6s, Iamsterdam, MK.* **Map** *p143 N11.*
Inaugurated in 1675, architect Elias Bouwman's mammoth synagogue is one of the largest in the world and was reputedly inspired by the Temple of Solomon. It is built on wooden piles and surrounded by smaller annexes (including offices, archives and one of the world's oldest libraries). The synagogue holds occasional concerts and candlelit events.

💜 Rembrandthuis

Jodenbreestraat 4 (520 0400, www.rembrandthuis.nl). Tram 9, 14 or Metro Waterlooplein. **Open** *10am-6pm daily.* **Admission** *€13; €4-€10 reductions; free under-6s, Iamsterdam, MK.* **Map** *p143 M10.*

Rembrandt bought this house in 1639 for 13,000 guilders (then a massive sum), at the height of his career. Sadly, the free-spending artist went bankrupt in 1656 and was forced to move to a smaller house (Rozengracht 184). The house on Jodenbreestraat is now a museum, whose faithfully reconstructed interiors are based on the room-by-room inventory of his possessions that was made when he went bankrupt. The museum also contains a remarkable collection of Rembrandt's etchings.

Tropenmuseum

Linnaeusstraat 2 (568 8200, www.tropenmuseum.nl). Tram 9, 14. **Open** *10am-5pm Tue-Sun.* **Admission** *€15; €8-€14 reductions; free under-4s, Iamsterdam, MK.* **Map** *p143 R12.*
Visitors to this handsome building get a vivid glimpse of daily life in the tropical and subtropical parts of the world – a strange evolution for a museum that was originally erected in the 1920s to glorify Dutch colonialism. Exhibits (which range from religious items and jewellery to washing powder and vehicles) are divided by region. Temporary shows, covering everything from Buddhism to Rhythm and Roots, are also consistently excellent. Children are made welcome too: a special branch of the museum, the Tropenmuseum Junior, is aimed at six- to 13-year-olds and has some inspired exhibitions of its own.

♥ Verzetsmuseum

Plantage Kerklaan 61 (620 2535, www.verzetsmuseum.org). Tram 9, 14. **Open** *10am-5pm Mon-Fri; 11am-5pm Sat, Sun.* **Admission** *€10; €5 reductions; free under-7s, Iamsterdam, MK.* **Map** *p143 P11.*
The Verzetsmuseum is one of Amsterdam's most illuminating museums, and quite possibly its most moving. It tells the story of the Dutch Resistance through a wealth of artefacts: false ID papers, clandestine printing presses, illegal newspapers, spy gadgets and an authentic secret door behind which Jews once hid. The engaging presentation is enhanced by the constant use of personal testimonies. Regularly changing temporary exhibitions explore various wartime themes and there's a small research room as well.

Restaurants & cafés

Beter & Leuk €€

Eerste Oosterparkstraat 91 (767 0029, www.beterenleuk.nl). Tram 3. **Open** *8.30am-5pm Mon-Fri; 9.30am-5pm Sat, Sun.* **Map** *p143 O15* ❶ *Café*
A breakfast-slash-lunch-slash-boutique café with a mission summed up by its name: 'Better & Nice'. Decoration is minimal and the kitchen open to view. The menu – including eggs, croissants, homemade granola, sandwiches, salads and cakes – is scribbled on a blackboard and handwritten on brown paper. The monthly Sunday vegan brunch is popular.

Louie Louie €€

Linnaeusstraat 11A (370 2981, www.louielouie.nl). Tram 9. **Open** *9am-1am Mon-Thur, Sun; 9am-3am Fri, Sat.* **Map** *p143 S12* ❷ *European*
Boasting a prime location right near the lush Oosterpark, Louie Louie is the perfect place for a spot of unashamed people-watching. In summer, the windows are opened so the cocktail-sipping patrons can spill out onto the large terrace. The brunch menu is delicious, and if you're dropping by for a pre-dinner drink be sure to try the beef tacos.

❤ La Rive €€€€

InterContinental Amstel Amsterdam, Professor Tulpplein 1 (520 3264, www.restaurantlarive. com). Tram 7, 10 or Metro Weesperplein. Open 6.30-10pm daily. Map p143 N14 ❸ *French*

Here you'll find superb regional French cuisine without the excessive formality that can too often mar such places. For the perfect meal when money is no object.

Woo Bros €€

Jodenbreestraat 144 (428 0488, www.woobros.nl). Tram 9, 14 or Metro Waterlooplein. Open 4pm-11pm Tue-Sun. Map p143 M10 ❹ *Asian*

With a menu of small dishes (three per person is about right for a full meal) that switches seamlessly from Japanese to Indonesian, Vietnamese to Thai, to Chinese and back (Peking duck sits alongside sushi), Woo Bros offers fusion perfection in quirky, low-lit surroundings.

Bars

De Biertuin

Linnaeusstraat 29 (665 0956, www.debiertuin. nl). Tram 9. Open 11am-1am Mon-Thur, Sun; 11am-3am Fri, Sat. Map p143 S13 ❶

The 'Beer Garden' does indeed have a wide selection of beers, as well as some of the city's most highly regarded grilled chicken. The proprietors also run other student- and hipster-friendly restaurant-bars in Oost, including the more appropriately liquor-soaked **Bukowski** (Oosterpark 10, 370 1685, www.barbukowski.nl).

❤ Brouwerij 't IJ

Funenkade 7 (528 6237, www. brouwerijhetij.nl). Tram 10. Open 2-8pm daily. Map p143 S11 ❷

Amsterdam is known for its microbrewery scene. There are dozens dotted throughout the city but most locals will argue Brouwerij 't IJ sets the standard, with tours and tastings, and its very own famous pub adjoining, where wares can be sampled. The award-winning local brewery is located at the base of the Gooyer windmill. The pub's interior still reflects its former function as the municipal baths and seating is minimal, so if the weather permits, head outside to the pavement tables. You'll recognise the brewery's label and logo – which features an ostrich with an egg and a distant windmill – from bars and restaurants around town.

Café de Sluyswacht

Jodenbreestraat 1 (625 7611, www. sluyswacht.nl). Tram 9, 14 or Metro Waterlooplein. Open 12.30pm-1am Mon-Thur; 12.30pm-3am Fri, Sat; 12.30pm-7pm Sun. Map p143 M10 ❸

Listing crazily, this wooden-framed bar has been pleasing drinkers for decades, though the building itself has been around since 1695, when it began life as a lock-keeper's cottage. It's snug and warm inside, while outside commands great views of Oude Schans – making it suitable for boozing in both balmy and inclement weather.

Hiding in Plain Sight

Rapenburg 18 (06 2529 3620 mobile, www.hpsamsterdam.com). Bus 22, 48. Open 6pm-1am Mon-Thur, Sun; 6pm-3am Fri, Sat. Map p143 N9 ❹

Given this speakeasy-style cocktail bar's proximity to the ancient docks where sailors would kiss their goodbyes before embarking on treacherous journeys, it's appropriate that it offers liquid

Koninklijk Theater Carré

danger in the form of a concoction called 'the Walking Dead'. Based on the potent zombie, served (and then set on fire) in a giant glass skull. Bar-imposed limit: one per night.

Shops & services

Ashes to Snow
Javastraat 72 (362 1480, www. ashestosnow.com). Tram 14. **Open** *10am-7pm Tue, Wed; 10am-9pm Thur, Fri; 10am-6pm Sat; noon-5pm Sun.* **Map** *p143* ❶ *Fashion*
For fashionistas who want a bit more from their shopping experience, high-end salon Ashes to Snow will certainly deliver. As well as a stunning collection of unique additions for your wardrobe, the versatile shop is also a gallery and gig venue for small musical performances. It often hosts pop-up stores and exhibits too, so expect the unexpected.

TunFun
Mr Visserplein 7 (689 4300, www. tunfun.nl). Tram 9, 14 or Metro Waterlooplein. **Open** *10am-6pm daily.* **Admission** *€8.50 1-12s; free adults.* **No cards.** **Map** *p143 N10* ❷ *Play centre*
An urban recycling success, this cavernous indoor playground used to be an underpass. Huge soft-play constructions provide endless joy for those under 12, with ball pools for tiny tots and full-on jungle gyms for older kids.

Waterlooplein
Waterlooplein (no phone). Tram 9, 14 or Metro Waterlooplein. **Open** *9am-5.30pm Mon-Fri; 8.30am-5.30pm Sat.* **No cards.** **Map** *p143 M10* ❸ *Market*
Amsterdam's top tourist market is basically an enormous flea market with the added attraction of loads of new clothes (although gear can be a bit pricey and, at many stalls,

a bit naff). Bargains can be found, but they may well be hidden under piles of cheap 'n' nasty toasters and down-at-heel (literally) shoes. Be prepared to dig around.

Entertainment

♥ Canvas

*Wibautstraat 150 (716 3817, www. volkshotel.nl/canvas). Tram 3 or Metro Wibautstaat. **Open** club 11pm-4am Fri, Sat. **Admission** varies. **Map** p143 O13* **❶** *Club*

Canvas's programme ranges from cutting-edge electronica through hip hop to club house and live jazz. Sitting atop a former newspaper-building-turned-hotel, it also sports some of the best views in town – along with the most hilarious toilet attendants. During the day, it operates as a café and cocktail bar.

Koninklijk Theater Carré

*Amstel 115-125 (0900 252 5255 premium rate, www.carre. nl). Tram 4, 7, 10 or Metro Weesperplein. **Box office** By phone 9am-9pm Mon-Fri; 10am-8pm Sat, Sun. In person 4-6pm or until start of performance daily. Tickets prices vary. **Map** p143 N13* **❷** *Theatre*

Many performers dream of appearing in this glamorous space, originally a 19th-century circus building refurbished in a grand style. The Carré hosts some of the best Dutch cabaret artists and touring operas, as well as the odd big music name. If musical theatre is your thing, this is the place to come for Dutch versions of popular blockbusters such as *Grease* and *Cats*. The annual World Christmas Circus brings in the world's classiest acts and clowns.

♥ Nationale Opera & Ballet

*Amstel 3 (625 8117 information, 625 5455 box office, www. operaballet.nl). Tram 9, 14 or Metro Waterlooplein. **Box office** noon-6pm Mon-Fri; noon-3pm Sat, Sun; or until start of performance. Tickets from €15. **Map** p143 M11* **❸** *Theatre*

Formerly called the Muziektheater, the building – and its primary tenants, the Dutch National Ballet and Dutch National Opera – was reborn as the Nationale Opera & Ballet back in 2014. The stage is used by leading dance companies on tour and to host the latest opera offering. It has a reputation for high-quality performances at good prices. Tickets go on sale three months in advance and often sell out fast, so it's advisable to book early.

Nationale Opera and Ballet

Waterfront & Noord

Amsterdam's historic wealth owes a lot to the waterfront: it was here that goods were unloaded and prepared for storage in the local warehouses. At one time, the harbour and its arterial canals was part of the city itself. But a drop in commerce slowly destabilised this unity, and the building of Centraal Station in the late 19th century served as a final marker of change.

These days the area is a showcase of pioneering architecture, and the green structure of the Renzo Piano-designed **NEMO** science museum dominates the horizon. It dwarfs the silver shell-shaped **ARCAM** architecture gallery as well as the nautically inclined **Nederlands Scheepvaartmuseum** and **Openbare Bibliotheek**

Morning power-up
Find a cure for caffeine
withdrawal at The Coffee Virus
(*p158*).

Adrenalin rush
Swing 'Over the Edge' from the
rooftop of A'DAM Toren (*p153*).

Best museum
Nederlands Scheepvaartmuseum
(*p156*) is one of the world's finest
nautical museums.

Entertain the kids
Keep kids happy with hands-on
trickery, gadgetry and tomfoolery
at NEMO Science Museum (*p156*).

Big screen
Enter a world of cinema at EYE
Film Institute (*p154*).

Eco-credentials
Eat local, organic food in Café de
Ceuvel (*p158*), built out of recycled
houseboats, or hang out at post-
industrial hub NDSM (*p160*).

Cultural fix
Muziekgebouw aan 't IJ (*p162*) for
contemporary classical music.

Drinking hotspot
Party on Hannekes Boom's (*p161*)
terrace overlooking the harbour,
or on Pllek's (*p161*) manmade
sandy beach.

Amsterdam (OBA), the largest library in the country, just
east of Centraal Station.

Eyes are also focused across the IJ on Noord.
Disregarded for decades, Noord was typified by derelict
docks and decrepit buildings. The turn of the 21st century
saw young creatives and families lured to the region by its
low rent. In recent years it has become the city's bastion of
alternative culture, with festivals, sustainable restaurants
and unrivalled views of the city. The latter is especially
true at **A'DAM Toren** – the 22-storey 'King of the Noord'
located next to the futuristic **EYE Film Institute**. Free
24-hour ferries unite the area with the rest of the city.

➡ **Getting around**
Buses 34, 35 and 763 run to Noord from Centraal Station, but the best
way to see the sights is by bicycle. Free ferries, which accommodate bikes,
run 24/7 from Centraal across to NDSM and Tolhuistuin. Tram 14 and
Metro Waterlooplein run from Centraal Station to the heart of the Eastern
Docklands; bus 22 goes via Zeeburg.

🖤 A'DAM Toren

*Overhoeksplein 1 (237 6310, www.adamtoren.nl). Bus 38 or Buiksloterweg ferry. **Open** 10am-1am Mon-Thur, Sun; 10am-3am Fri, Sat (hours vary for restaurant, bar and Lookout – check website for details). **Map** p154 M5.*

You can spot it from a mile (or more) away. Standing tall in Amsterdam's trendiest neighbourhood, the A'DAM Toren has been hailed the 'King of the Noord'. Perched directly across the IJ from Centraal Station, it is the pinnacle of the area's post-industrial revival in every sense of the word. It opened in 2016 as a cultural hub for creatives, culinary enthusiasts and clubbers. And while it may look shiny and new, the tower's 22 storeys have decades of tales to tell.

The landmark dates back to 1971 as the home of multinational oil company Royal Dutch Shell. Designed by architect Arthur Staal, it was known as Shelltoren by Amsterdammers until 2009, when the company's headquarters relocated.

Almost a decade and a multi-million-euro refit later, the building reopened. The very existence of A'DAM Toren is a big nod to how much the city values art and culture. There were much higher bids placed for the building, but the municipality chose the vision for a vertical city with 'wow' factor over standard accounting, investment and law firms.

On the top floor, at almost 100 metres (330 feet) above ground, its 360° observation deck offers panoramic views of the city. For daredevils, **A'DAM Lookout** has the highest swing in Europe, which lets riders swoop dramatically over the 17th-century skyline. The tower is also home to **Moon**, the high-end restaurant that revolves as you eat (*see p159*), **MA'ADAM** skybar on the top floor, **A'DAM Music School** for locals to brush up on their talents, and **Shelter** – a 24-hour club in the basement. Want to try it all? Spend a night or two in **Sir Adam**, the Tower's urban boutique hotel.

WATERFRONT & NOORD

Sights & museums

ARCAM

Prins Hendrikkade 600 (620 4878, www.arcam.nl). Bus 22. **Open** *1-5pm Tue-Sun.* **Admission** *free.* **Map** *p154 P9.*

The gallery at the Architecture Centrum Amsterdam is obsessed with the promotion of Dutch contemporary architecture, from the early 20th-century creations of the world-famous Amsterdam School to more modern designs. It organises forums, lectures, its own series of architecture books, and exhibitions in its fresh 'silver snail' location.

❤ EYE Film Institute

IJPromenade 1 (589 1400, www. eyefilm.nl). Bus 38 or Buiksloterweg ferry. **Open** *Exhibitions 10am-7pm daily. Box office 10am-10pm daily.* **Map** *p154 M4.*

If you've been in the city for a day, chances are you've already spied the EYE Film Institute. With a futuristic angular design, the origami-like structure – which looks as though it might take flight at any moment – is pretty hard to miss. With four film theatres, a quirky gift shop and an exhibition space, the EYE has been drawing crowds across the IJ since it opened in 2012. It could be due to its 700-square-metre (7,530-square-feet) bar-restaurant with a wrap-around waterside terrace, or the variety of art and musical events it hosts year-round. Exhibitions cover directors such as Tacita Dean, urban ecologist Martin Melchers and local hero Johan van der Keuken, with related programming taking place in the cinemas. Downstairs, there are pods in which you can surf through the history of Dutch film.

▶ *The EYE hosts the Cinedans festival (see p59) and the KLIK! animation festival (see p63).*

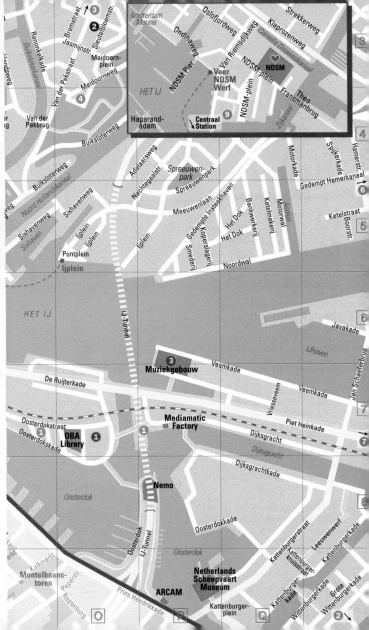

NEMO

Mediamatic Factory

Dijksgracht 6 (638 9901, www. mediamatic.net). Tram 26. **Open** *varies.* **Admission** *varies.* **Map** *p154 P7.*

Mediamatic Factory is a project/ exhibition space and hydroponic farm in an ancient warehouse. It's home to an inspired multimedia team, who pop up all over the place with all sorts of inspired projects. From an interactive urinal installation that creates fertilizer for its park to an exhibition of pimped-up pig hearts, it's almost impossible to guess what's next up the Mediamatic sleeve.

♥ Nederlands Scheepvaartmuseum

Kattenburgerplein 1 (523 2222, www.hetscheepvaartmuseum. nl). Bus 22. **Open** *9am-5pm daily.* **Admission** *€15; €7.50 reductions; free under-4s, Iamsterdam, MK.* **Map** *p154 P9.*

Dutch nautical history is rich and fascinating, so it follows that the country should boast one of the world's finest maritime museums – second only, say experts, to London's National Maritime Museum. Marvel at the models, portraits, boat parts and other naval ephemera, housed in a wonderful building built 350 years ago by Daniel Stalpaert. Don't miss the large replica of an 18th-century East India Trading Company (VOC) ship, with costumed 'sailors'.

♥ NEMO Science Center

Oosterdok 2 (531 3233, www.e-nemo.nl). Bus 22, 48. **Open** *10am-5.30pm Tue-Sun. School holidays 9am-5.30pm daily.* **Admission** *€16.50; €8.25 reductions; free under-4s, Iamsterdam, MK.* **Map** *p154 P8.*

NEMO has built a strong reputation as a child-friendly science museum. It eschews exhibits in favour of all manner of hands-on trickery, gadgetry and tomfoolery: you can play DNA detective games, blow mega soap bubbles or explode things in a 'wonderlab'. The building itself, designed by Renzo Piano to look like a mammoth copper-green ship's hull, is a true eye-pleaser. The rooftop café is a lovely place in which to while away an afternoon – that is, if it's not being used as a virtual beach or for a jazz festival.

OBA (Openbare Bibliotheek Amsterdam)

Oosterdokskade 143 (523 0900, www.oba.nl). Tram 1, 2, 4, 5, 9, 13, 16, 17, 26. **Open** *10am-10pm daily.* **Admission** *free.* **Map** *p154 O8.*
This big city landmark opened on 07-07-07 and has since become one of Amsterdam's most treasured architectural gems. Designed by Jo Coenen, the former state architect of the Netherlands, OBA treats arriving visitors to a soaring view up to its top floor café-restaurant, which, in turn, offers a spectacular view over Amsterdam. The interior, with walnut floors and white walls and shelves, is low-key; colour comes from the books and mixed bag of people using the free Wi-Fi – or the polyester study 'pods'.

Visitors can take their pick from 600 internet-connected computers, 50 multimedia workplaces, 110 catalogue reference terminals and almost a dozen print and copy stations. These are accompanied by a theatre, exhibition space, music department and a radio station.

Tolhuistuin

IJ Promenade 2 (760 4820, www.tolhuistuin.nl). Ferry 901. **Open** *10am-10pm daily (kitchen 11am-4pm, 5.30-10pm).* **Map** *p154 M5.*
A former Shell-site-turned-cultural-playground, Tolhuistuin (Toll House) definitely fits Noord's achingly trendy bill. With prime real estate directly across the IJ from Centraal Station, Tolhuistuin is the perfect hangout spot on a warm sunny day. Within the precinct is a concert hall, exhibition space and café-restaurant complete with outdoor terrace and hammocks.

Restaurants & cafés

&Samhoud Places €€€€

Oosterdokskade 5 (260 2094, www. samhoudplaces.com). Tram 1, 2, 4, 5, 9, 13, 16, 17, 26. **Open** *Restaurant 7pm-9.30pm Wed, Thur, Sat; noon-2pm, 7pm-9.30pm Fri; noon-2pm, 7pm-8.30pm Sun.* **Map** *p154 N7*
❶ *Global*
Bringing gastronomy to Amsterdam, &Samhoud Places is one of the most insanely

Nederlands Scheepvaartmuseum

popular (and expensive) high-end restaurants in town – complete with two Michelin stars. If your budget won't stretch that far, you can settle in the lounge for a cocktail and a rather more affordable tomato burger.

1e Klas €€€

Centraal Station, Platform 2B (625 0131, www.restaurant1eklas.nl). Tram 1, 2, 4, 5, 9, 13, 14, 16, 17, 24. **Open** *8.30am-11pm daily.* **Map** *p154 M7* ❷ *Brasserie/pub*

This former brasserie for first-class commuters is now open to anyone who wants to kill some time in style – with a full meal, snack or drink – while waiting for a train. The art nouveau interior will whisk you straight back to the 1890s. The adjoining pub is also a treat and hosts regular jazz concerts.

❤ Café de Ceuvel €€

Korte Papaverweg 4 (229 6210, www.deceuvel.nl). Bus 34, 35 or Builsloterweg ferry. **Open** *11am-midnight Tue-Thur, Sun; 11am-2am Fri, Sat.* **Map** *p154 O1* ❸ *Dutch*

Amsterdam's sustainable culture extends beyond architecture and – with a menu based on locally sourced, seasonal produce – Café de Ceuvel is the perfect example. The restaurant is part of the award-winning De Ceuvel complex, a former shipyard revived using recycled materials. It even sells fresh produce from its rooftop farm.

Café Modern €€

Meidoornweg 2 (494 0684, www.modernamsterdam.nl). Bus 38 or Builsloterweg ferry. **Open** *7pm-1am Mon, Tue; noon-3pm, 7pm-1am Wed-Sat.* **Map** *p154 O4* ❹ *Global*

By day, this old bank building is brunch spot **Jacques Jour**. By night, under the name Café Modern, this roomy and wittily designed space is a globe-trotting

restaurant serving a set menu; book in advance. Upstairs is boutique hotel **Sweet Dreamz** (www. sweetdreamz.nl).

❤ The Coffee Virus €€

Overhoeksplein 2 (2870 9872, www.thecoffeevirus.nl). Bus 38 or Buiksloterweg ferry. **Open** *9am-4.30pm Mon-Fri.* **Map** *p154 M4* ❺ *Café*

Creative types flock to this canteen, which has two espresso roasts and three filter coffee roasts that rotate regularly. There's also good sandwiches and salads.

Hangar €€

Aambeeldstraat 36 (363 8657, www.hangar.amsterdam). Bus

33. **Open** *10am-1pm Mon-Thur, Sun; 10am-3am Fri, Sat.* **Map** *p154 R5* 6 *South European*
A self-described 'beautiful mess', the aptly named Hangar has warmed up an old hangar with a tropical-inspired interior.

Koffiehuis KHL €€
Oostelijke Handelskade 44 (779 1575, www.khl.nl). Tram 10, 26. **Open** *11.30am-1am Tue-Sat, 11.30am-midnight Sun.* **Map** *p154 R7* 7 *European*
The beautiful, light-flooded interior harks back to the days in the early 20th century when this was a canteen serving staff of the Royal Holland Lloyd shipping line. Now it's a café-cum-meeting space serving the local community, with plenty to attract new visitors. There's art on the walls and regular live music to lift the spirits.

Moon €€€€
A'DAM Toren, Overhoeksplein 1 (237 6310, restaurantmoon. nl). Ferry 901. **Open** *6pm-late Mon-Thur; noon-late Fri-Sun.* *p154 M5* 8 *Global*
If you're able to splash out on one memorable experience during your stay, Moon will undoubtedly deliver. Perched on the 19th-floor of the A'DAM Toren, its revolving floor proffers guests 360° panoramic views of the city, without having to leave the table. It's fine dining with a twist. Literally.

💜 NDSM

Neveritaweg 61 (493 1070, www. NDSM.nl). Bus 35 or ferry 906. **Open** *9am-5pm Mon-Fri.* **Map** *p154 inset.*

A 20-minute free ferry ride from Centraal Station, the former shipyard NDSM-werf sports a unique post-apocalyptic vibe that's ideal for parties, concerts and wacky theatre festivals. One hall forms the country's largest cultural incubator, with over 100 studios for artists, theatre companies and other creative professionals. The interior walls of this Kunststad ('Art City', as it's now known) give the feeling of an expressionist film set.

As ground zero for Dutch subculture, NDSM has attracted some big players. TV network MTV set up its Benelux headquarters in a revamped former woodwork factory; Greenpeace moved its offices here (handy for parking its boat *Sirius*); and even the iconic Dutch department store HEMA is headquartered here, complete with a flagship shop (NDSM-straat 12) to test new products and services. One of NDSM's most impressive assets is **Crane Hotel Faralda** (*see p175*): the high-end mini hotel is situated in a crane once used to drag ships to dry dock; it's now a private hotspot for DJs, VIPs and even royals.

To complete the picture of an alternative area where hippie ideals meet high tech, visit the **Noorderlicht Café** (NDSM Plein 102, 492 2770, www. noorderlichtcafe.nl), which offers a rustic vibe: there's a campfire, lounge music, strings of colourful lights and a terrace. Two minutes away is urban beach hotspot **Pllek**, which is built, appropriately enough, out of shipping containers (*see p161*). Recycling has indeed come a long way – what's described above is only the tip of the post-industrial iceberg.

Hannekes Boom

❤ Pllek €€
Neveritaweg 59 (290 0020, www.
pllek.nl). Bus 35, 37, 38 or ferry
906. **Open** *9.30am-1am Mon-*
Thur, Sun; 9.30am-3am Fri, Sat.
Kitchen closes 10pm daily. **Map** *p154*
inset ❾ *Global*

Surrounded by the cultural melting
pot that is NDSM, Pllek is the
product of a recycled warehouse
and some shipping containers.
The affordable set menu features
seasonal and sustainable
ingredients for less than €30 for
three courses.

During summer, the man-made
urban beach – which overlooks
Amsterdam from across the IJ – is
inundated with sun-seekers, and
in the winter a huge bonfire keeps

patrons warm. The venue also
hosts DJs and major music events,
including the city's notorious ADE
(Amsterdam Dance Event) and
has opened the hall next to the
restaurant as a live music venue,
Pllek Live Stage.

Bars

❤ Hannekes Boom
Dijksgracht 4 (419 9820, www.
hannekesboom.nl). Tram 26.
Open *11am-1am Mon-Thur, Sun;*
11am-3am Fri, Sat. **Map** *p154 P7* ❶

With a huge terrace and a view of
the harbour, the shack-style Boom
rates as one of the city's hottest
hotspots – even though it is made
of scrap lumber. Not only street-art
friendly, it also has live music and
DJ nights.

Roest
Jacob Bontiusplaats, entrance on
Czar Peterstraat 213 (308 0283,
www.amsterdamroest.nl). Tram
10, 26 or bus 22. **Open** *4pm-1am*
Thur; 4pm-3am Fri; noon-3am
Sat, noon-11pm Sun. Exceptions for
events. **Map** *p154 R9* ❷

In the know
Lock stop

If you're exploring Noord via bike, it's
always worth stopping at the ancient
Café 't Sluisje (Nieuwendammerdijk
297, 636 1712, www.cafehetsluisje.
nl), with its terrace straddling a lock
system in Nieuwendam, the oldest
part of Noord.

Named 'rust' as a nod to its industrial setting, Roest has plenty of middle-of-nowhere, graffiti-covered credentials. Its line-up of ever-changing themed parties, not to mention the expansive outdoor terrace and sandy beach, manage to keep even the most fickle trendsters entertained. It throws larger parties in the industrial Van Gendthallen across the way.

Shops & services

Blom & Blom

Chrysantenstraat 20 (737 2691, www.blomandblom.com). Bus 34, 35, 38 or ferry 901. **Open** *10am-6pm Tue-Fri; 11am-5pm Sat.* **Map** *p154 N3* ❶ *Homewares*
Industrial home deco at its finest – interior fanatics with no space in their suitcase should approach Blom & Blom with caution. The minimalist white-space interior is decorated with exposed industrial lamps and wooden furnishings, all of which are available for purchase, along with cooler-than-cool accessories.

Pekmarkt

EC Van der Pekstraat (737 1412). Bus 32, 33, 34, 35, 38 or Buiksloterweg ferry. **Open** *9am-5pm Wed, Fri, Sat.* **Map** *p154 O3* ❷ *Market*
With an array of fresh produce and unique trinkets, Pekmarkt is a veritable treasure trove. There's a special organic market on Fridays, and on Saturdays vintage sellers come out to play.

Entertainment

Conservatorium van Amsterdam

Oosterdokskade 151 (527 7550, www.ahk.nl/conservatorium). Tram 1, 2, 4, 5, 9, 13, 16, 17, 26. **Open** *times vary. Tickets prices vary.* **Map** *p154 O8* ❶ *Live music*

Concerts and presentations take place almost daily, and often for free, in the Amsterdam Conservatory's gorgeous glass building east of Centraal Station. You'll find everything here, from classical quartets to jazz big bands.

🖤 Muziekgebouw aan 't IJ

Piet Heinkade 1 (788 2000, www.muziekgebouw.nl). Tram 26. **Box office** *noon-6pm Mon-Sat. Tickets prices vary.* **Map** *p154 P7* ❷ *Live music*
Designed by the Danish architectural practice 3xNielsen, the Muziekgebouw is one of the most innovative musical complexes in Europe, befitting its previous incarnation as the IJsbreker, whose ethos was to promote modern variants of classical, jazz and world music. Never afraid to take risks, the centre's schedule ranges from cutting-edge multimedia works to celebrations of composers from the last 150 years. It's also home to the Klankspeeltuin – where seven- to 12-year-olds can play with an inspired selection of musical machines – and also the ever-popular **Bimhuis** jazz club.

Shelter

Overhoeksplein 3 (www.shelteramsterdam.nl). Builsloterweg Ferry 901. **Open** *11pm-8am Fri, Sat.* **Admission** *varies.* **Map** *p154 M5* ❸ *Club*
Set in the basement of A'DAM Toren (*see p153*) and boasting a coveted 24-hour licence, this is underground clubbing at its finest. The venue opened its doors in October 2016, and has since housed an impressive line-up of big-shot DJs on its decks. If you plan to take advantage of its insomniac-friendly opening hours, refuel upstairs at **The Butcher Social Club**, which is also open 24/7.

Sarphatipark p165

De Pijp

You don't come to De Pijp for historical sites; this area is rooted firmly in the present. Well over 150 different nationalities keep its global village feeling alive, and many upmarket restaurants and bars have flourished here in recent years. The gentrification process is firmly under way as the construction of the Metro's controversial Noord-Zuidlijn continues pretty much directly beneath bustling Ferdinand Bolstraat.

De Pijp is the best known of the working-class quarters built in the late 19th century. Harsh economic times necessitated a plan of long, narrow streets, leading to its apt nickname, 'the Pipe'. High rents forced tenants to sublet rooms to students and artists, lending the area its bohemian character.

Start the day
Lounge at loft café CT Coffee & Coconuts (*p167*).

Best bargains
Hit the neighbourhood-defining Albert Cuypmarkt (*p168*) street market.

Shoppers' paradise
Hutspot Amsterdam (*p170*) is a department store of pop-up shops.

Top-floor cocktails
Raise a glass to the view at Twenty Third Bar (*p169*).

Cosy coffeeshop
Some say Katsu (*p170*) has the best selection of weed in town.

Escape the buzz
Slip off for a picnic in friendly local Sarphatipark (*p165*).

Today, De Pijp is home to a mix of halal butchers, Surinamese, Spanish and Turkish delicatessens, and restaurants offering authentic Syrian, Moroccan, Thai, Pakistani, Chinese and Indian cuisine. This makes it one of the best spots in town for quality snacking treats, the many ingredients for which are almost always bought fresh from the single largest daily market anywhere in the Netherlands: **Albert Cuypmarkt**. The market attracts thousands of customers every day to the junctions of Sweelinckstraat, Ferdinand Bolstraat and 1e Van der Helststraat, north into the lively Gerard Douplein, and also south towards **Sarphatipark**. Another pretty street, which is rich with cafés and bars, is Frans Halsstraat.

→ **Getting around**
Trams 4, 9, 16 and 24 run from Centraal Station to Albert Cuypstraat in the heart of De Pijp. Lines 3 and 12 also run between the east and western sides of the city through the neighbourhood. Key destinations in the area are easily walkable: Albert Cuypmarkt is a five-minute walk from the Heineken Experience.

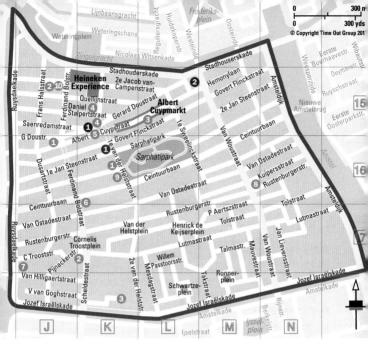

Sights & museums

Heineken Experience

Stadhouderskade 78 (523 9666, www.heinekenexperience. com). Tram 7, 10, 16, 24. **Open** *10.30am-7.30pm Mon-Thur; 10.30am-9pm Fri-Sun. Last ticket sale 2hrs before closing.* **Admission** *€16; €12.50 reductions; free under 11s.* **Map** *p165 K15.*

Heineken stopped brewing here in 1988, but kept the building open for tours. The 'experience' is spread across four levels, with interactive displays, a mini brewery and a stable walk, where visitors can see Heineken's iconic shire horses. And where else can you take a virtual reality ride from the perspective of a Heineken bottle? Plus you get three cold ones at the end.

♥ Sarphatipark

Sarphatipark (664 1350, www. sarphatipark.wordpress.com). Tram 3 or 25. **Open** *daily.* **Admission** *free.* **Map** *p165 L16.*

Sarphatipark occupies two blocks in the middle of the district. It is named after the doctor and philanthropist Samuel Sarphati, who is remembered with a monument and fountain. Sarphati showed philanthropic tendencies as a baker of inexpensive bread for the masses, and as initiator of the city's rubbish collection. The park was designed in the English landscape style and was opened in 1886, almost two decades after its namesake's death. Today, it is populated by young families, picnicking locals and cycling tourists.

The Butcher

Restaurants

Albina €
*Albert Cuypstraat 69 (675 5135).
Tram 16, 24.* **Open** *10.30am-10pm
Tue-Sun.* **No cards**. *Map p165
J16* ❶ *Asian*
One in a whole row of cheap Suri-
Chin-Indo spots located in De Pijp,
Albina – where a Chinese influence
predominates – gets top marks for
its lightning service and reliable
vegetarian or meat meals with roti,
rice or noodles.

Bakers & Roasters €€
*Eerste Jacob van Campenstraat 54
(772 2627, www.bakersandroasters.
com). Tram 4, 12, 16.* **Open**
*8.30am-4pm daily. Map p165
J15* ❷ *Café*
The brainchild of a Brazilian and
New Zealander, Bakers & Roasters
delivers brunch favourites in
generous quantities. Come with
enough room for a main course and
a peanut butter smoothie, but be
warned, it doesn't take bookings

and the waiting list can be up to an
hour long. Visit between Monday
and Wednesday, and get there early.

Bazar €
*Albert Cuypstraat 182 (675 0544,
www.bazaramsterdam.nl). Tram
16, 24.* **Open** *10am-midnight daily.*
Map *p165 L15* ❸ *North African*
This former church, now an Arabic-
kitsch café, is one of the glories
of Albert Cuypmarkt. Sticking
to the winning formula set by its
Rotterdam mothership, the menu
lingers in North Africa.

Brut de Mer €€
*Gerard Douplein 811 (471 4099,
www.brutdemer.nl). Tram 3,
4, 12, 16.* **Open** *4pm-11pm Mon-
Thur; 1pm-11pm Fri-Sun. Map p165
K15* ❹ *Seafood*
The gentrification of De Pijp saw an
influx of trendy restaurant and café
concepts popping up next to street
food vendors. One of these is Brut
de Mer, which was the first seafood
joint in the area when it opened

in 2015. It's been a raging success ever since. You can't go wrong with oysters and bubbles.

The Butcher €€
Albert Cuypstraat 129 (470 7875, www.the-butcher.com). Tram 4, 16, 24. **Open** *noon-11pm Mon, Tue, Sun; noon-1am Wed, Thur; noon-3am Fri, Sat.* **Map** *p165 K15* ⑤ *Burgers*

It's all about the burgers at this chic-but-spare joint. About a dozen versions are on offer, from aptly titled The Daddy (250g prime Aberdeen Angus beef) to the Veggie Delight. If the Butcher is full, try **Burgermeester** at no.48 (www.burgermeester.eu), an outlet of the citywide healthy burger chain.

❤ CT Coffee & Coconuts €€
Ceintuurbaan 282 (354 1104, www.ctamsterdam.nl). Tram 3, 4, 12, 16. **Open** *8am-11pm daily.* **Map** *p165 K16* ⑥ *Café*

A former movie cinema, this four-storey loft café retains its classic exterior. Inside, sofas line exposed-brick walls and rope suspends candlelit tables from the high ceiling. It's a buzzing spot, where the city's creatives come to caffeinate. CT's menu is a reflection of its vacation-inspired atmosphere. The coconut coffee is a must for anyone with a sweet tooth, and the scrambled eggs avo is its perfect savoury accompaniment.

The Fat Dog €
Ruysdaelkade 251 (221 6249, www.thefatdog.nl). Tram 4, 12, 16. **Open** *noon-midnight Wed-Sun.* **Map** *p165 J17* ⑦ *American*

Placing a glutenous spin on the hot dog, The Fat Dog is the ideal place to slay an appetite. Its menu options include the all-pork Chinatown and the Roy Donders, which ditches the 'fancy' garnish in favour of just sausage with bread. It also has an excellent, but affordable, selection of champagne on the menu, because why not?

CT Coffee & Coconuts

❤ Albert Cuypmarkt

Albert Cuypstraat (no phone).
Tram 4, 16, 24. **Open** *9.30am-*
5.30pm Mon-Sat. **No cards.** *Map*
p165 L15.

This vast and busy street
market is definitely one for
the locals or visitors keen to
break free of the *grachts*. Once
a 19th-century development
for the working class, it's now
populated by Dutch, Moroccan,
Surinamese, Vietnamese and
Turkish stallholders. You'll find
everything from walls of veg, fresh
stroopwafels (the gooey, syrupy
Dutch treat) and Edam cheese to
Vietnamese *loempias* (spring rolls)
and Turkish flatbreads all being
hawked loudly by enthusiastic
vendors. Besides the food and the
regular market tat – nylon lingerie
that errs on the porno side,
knock-off perfumes (Guggi Envy,
anyone?), and a whole spectrum
of textiles, from faux Andy Warhol
prints to tan-coloured corduroy
– one of the biggest draws to dear
old Albert are the florists selling
ten white roses for €5 or bunches

of tulips for €1.50. If you go at the
end of the day, you may even score
some for free before marketeers
discard them. Attracting
thousands of customers six days
a week, Albert Cuypmarkt spills
merrily into the adjoining roads:
the junctions of Sweelinckstraat,
Ferdinand Bolstraat and 1e Van
der Helststraat, north into the
lively Gerard Douplein, and south
towards Sarphatipark.

While it's easy to get distracted
by all the stalls, it's worth checking
out the nearby shops and cafés.
For example, the charming and
helpful **Fourniturenwinkel Jan
De Grote Kleinvakman** (Albert
Cuypstraat 203a, 673 8247) – which
translates as 'Haberdashery Shop
Jan the Big Small Craftsman' – has
everything you need to keep your
wardrobe in good repair. You can
also check if the concept behind
Trust (Albert Cuypstraat 210,
737 1532) is still making business
sense: you pay what you want for
its fine selection of coffees, soups,
salads and sandwiches. Don't they
know how the marketplace works?

Firma Pekelhaaring €€
Van Woustraat 127 (679 0460,
www.pekelhaaring.nl). Tram 3, 4.
Open *10am-midnight daily.* **Map**
p165 M16 **8** *European*
Meat and fish dominate the
menu here – the grilled mackerel
is recommended – although
vegetarians will be happy with the
creative pasta dishes. Desserts are
also exemplary.

Scandinavian Embassy €€€
Sarphatipark 34 (61951 8199,
scandinavianembassy.nl). Tram 3,
4, 16, 24. **Open** *7.30am-6pm Mon-*
Fri; 9am-6pm Sat, Sun. **Map** *p165*
K16 **9** *Scandinavian*
Scandinavians know how to master
the finer things in life, including
fashion, food and coffee. This
place combines all three, and very
well at that. Set in a cosy space
overlooking Sarphatipark, the
menu features breakfast and lunch
options accompanied by the latest
fashion collections on display.

De Taart van m'n Tante €
Ferdinand Bolstraat 10 (776 4600,
www.detaart.com). Tram 3, 12,
16, 24. **Open** *10am-6pm daily.* **No**
cards. **Map** *p165 J15* **10** *Tearoom*
'My Aunt's Cake' started life as a
purveyor of over-the-top cakes
before becoming the campest
tearoom in town. In a glowing
pink space filled with mismatched
furniture, it's particularly
gay-friendly.

Bars

Boca's Park
Sarphatipark 4 (675 9945, www.
bar-bocas.nl) Tram 3, 4, 16, 24.
Open *10am-1am Mon-Thur;*
10am-3am Fri, Sat. **Map** *p165*
K16 **1**
Following the success of its first
location on Westerstraat, Boca's
Park perfects the bar-meets-mixed-
dining concept. The varied plates
are designed for sharing, and
complement the extensive wine list
with thirst-inducing precision.

Brouwerij Troost
Cornelis Trootsplein 21 (737 1028,
www.brouwerijtroost.nl). Tram
3, 12. **Open** *4pm-1am Mon-Thur;*
4pm-3am Fri; 2pm-3am Sat;
2pm-midnight Sun. **Map** *p165*
K17 **2**
If you don't have the energy to
battle crowds at the Heineken
Experience, why not visit De Pijp's
first official brewery instead?
Troost opened its doors in 2014,
much to the delight of locals and
has a tasting room and pub on site.

♥ Twenty Third Bar
Hotel Okura, Ferdinand Bolstraat
333 (678 7111, www.okura.nl).
Tram 12. **Open** *6pm-1am Mon-*
Thur, Sun; 6pm-2am Fri, Sat. **Map**
p165 K18 **3**
On the 23rd floor of Hotel Okura,
this cocktail and champagne bar
offers fantastic views of De Pijp and
the compact Amsterdam School
architecture of the Rivierenbuurt.
Be prepared to pay for the view –
cocktails start at €15 a pop and the
sommelier-selected champagne
and wine don't come cheap either.
If you're feeling particularly flush,
try the hotel's excellent (but
expensive) Japanese restaurant
Yamazato (678 7450).

Wijnbar Boelen & Boelen
1e Van der Helststraat 50 (671 2242,
www.wijnbar.nl). Tram 3, 4, 16,
24. **Open** *4pm-midnight Tue-Thur,*
Sun; 4pm-1am Fri; 3pm-1am Sat.
Map *p165 K15* **4**
Many people come here for the
Frenchified food, but, as the
name implies, wine is the star at
this compact yet airy bar on the
edge of De Pijp's main nightlife
strip. Dozens are available by the
glass, more by the bottle, and
prices range from pocket-friendly
to splurge.

Coffeeshops

♥ Katsu

Eerste van der Helststraat 70 (no phone, www.katsu.nl). Tram 3, 16, 24. **Open** *10am-midnight Mon-Thur; 10am-1am Fri, Sat; 11am-midnight.* **No cards. Map** *p165 K16* ❶

This little treasure offers a giant selection of various strains of hash and weed at a wide and fair range of prices – quite possibly the best selection in town, in fact. The interior is pleasantly green, with plenty of leafy potted plants, and a crowd of older locals.

Shops & services

Anna + Nina

Gerard Doustraat 94 (204 4532, www.anna-nina.nl). Tram 4, 16, 24. **Open** *noon-6pm Mon; 10am-6pm Tue-Fri; 11am-6pm Sat, Sun.* **Maps** *p165 K15* ❶ *Homewares*

This charming concept store provides a variety of quirky and unique pieces for the home. Specialising in botanical-inspired and rustic collections, Anna + Nina is definitely a cut above other interior stores.

♥ Hutspot Amsterdam

Van Woustraat 4 (223 1331, www. hutspot.com). Tram 4. **Open** *10am-7pm Mon-Sat; noon-6pm Sun.* **Map** *p165 L15* ❷ *Market*

A hipster's ideal consumer concept: a permanent place for pop-ups. Hutspot brings together 50 creatives dealing in all sorts of things, from furniture to sausages. Everything is for sale and the selection changes every month, so you can browse and snack happy. On the top floor, a café – with fantastic coffee – awaits.

Hutspot Amsterdam

DE PIJP

Amsterdam
Essentials

Accommodation

With accommodation options in the city running the gamut from B&Bs and privately owned small hotels to enormous, posh establishments, Amsterdam does its best to find a bed for everybody. The question of where to put new hotels in this densely packed environment has driven some creative and inspired solutions, from updating a youth prison to building designer suites in a crane. Limited space in the city centre means that hotel rooms there tend to be on the small side. But many make up for their somewhat modest dimensions with that most prized commodity: a canal view.

The Museum Quarter and the Grachtengordel have plenty of hotels, whereas De Pijp and the Jordaan are a good bet for private apartment rentals. In general, avoid accommodation near Centraal Station or the Red Light District, unless you want to be overcharged.

For the cheapest deals, your best bet will be to look online. Check out www.booking.nl and www.tripadvisor. com for seasonal and last-minute deals. The room rate may, or may not, include the city tax of five per cent. And note that credit cards aren't always accepted, particularly in smaller places.

The best way to experience Dutch hospitality is to stay in a B&B. These are often stylish affairs, with prices to match; www.bedandbreakfast.amsterdam is a good place to start. If you want to rent a houseboat for your stay, check out www.houseboats.nl.

In the know
Price categories

Our price categories are based on hotels' standard prices (not including seasonal offers or discounts) for one night in a double room with en suite.

Luxury	€300+
Expensive	€200-€300
Moderate	€100-€200
Budget	up to €100

Luxury

Conservatorium

Van Baerlestraat 27, Museum Quarter, (570 0000, www.conservatoriumhotel. com). Tram 2, 3, 5, 12, 16. **Map** *p129 G14.*

Located on the Museumplein, this grand 19th-century neo-Gothic building, latterly the Sweelinck music conservatory, has been transformed into a stylish place to stay. Italian architect Piero Lissoni has embraced the building's rich heritage while introducing contemporary clean lines and a muted colour scheme to the 129 rooms. As well as the ultra-luxe suites and spa and gym facilities, there's some excellent drinking and dining to be had. The Brasserie & Lounge is a striking space, with soaring windows and a glass ceiling.

Hotel de l'Europe

Nieuwe Doelenstraat 2-14, Old Centre (531 1777, www.deleurope.nl). Tram 4, 9, 14, 16. **Map** *p72 K11.*

A luxury landmark with fabulous views across the Amstel, this is the place to head for an indulgent splurge or a honeymoon hideaway. As should be expected at these prices, every detail is taken care of. The Provocateur suite has a round bed and an in-room Jacuzzi big enough for two. The hotel is one of the few in Amsterdam to boast a pool, and its Bord'Eau restaurant, with two Michelin stars, is highly rated. Freddy's Bar – named after beer king Heineken – is a woody and evocative place in which to sip a cocktail.

Hotel Pulitzer

Prinsengracht 315-331, Grachtengordel (523 5235, www. hotelpulitzeramsterdam.nl). Tram 13, 14, 17. **Map** *p97 H9.*

Sprawling across 25 canal houses, the Pulitzer is an ideal destination for an indulgent getaway. Guests can arrive by boat, there are antiques galore, rooms are big and stylish, and the facilities are top-notch. A lovely garden nestles at the back. In August, the Grachtenfestival (*see p62*) of classical music takes place

in and around the hotel grounds, making it an excellent choice for music fans.

Sofitel Legend The Grand Amsterdam

Oudezijds Voorburgwal 197, Old Centre (555 3111, www.sofitel-legend-thegrand. com). Tram 1, 2, 4, 5, 9, 13, 14, 16, 17. **Map** *p72 L9.*

Steeped in centuries of history, The Grand is located in the Red Light District. But the moment guests step into the luxurious courtyard, they feel a million miles away from the risqué surroundings. Rooms are spacious and airy, and there's also a stellar restaurant, Bridges (*see p80*).

Waldorf Astoria Amsterdam

Herengracht 542, Grachtengordel (718 4600, www.waldorfastoria3.hilton. com). Tram 4, 9. **Map** *p109 L12.*

Spanning a collection of six 17th-century canal palaces, the Waldorf Astoria definitely falls into the 'treat yourself' category. In addition to decadently decorated rooms, the hotel has its own courtyard garden and quintessential Amsterdam canal views.

W Hotel Amsterdam

Spuistraat 175, Old Centre (811 2500, www.wamsterdam.com). Tram 1, 13, 14, 17 or Metro 51, 53, 54. **Map** *p72 J9.*

Split across two buildings on the western edge of the Old Centre, this smart hotel delivers all of the luxury one would expect from the W Hotels group. Don't be fooled by the unassuming brown brick exterior. The inside boasts an intriguing mix of design, which combines influence from the city's heritage with upscale contemporary style. The rooftop bar, MR PORTER (*see p93*) offers incredible views of the city's 17th-century skyline and is open to all.

Expensive

Doubletree by Hilton

Oosterdoksstraat 4, Waterfront (530 0800, www.doubletree3.hilton.com). Tram 1, 2, 4, 5, 9, 13, 16, 17, 26. **Map** *p154 N7.*

Just east of Centraal Station near the OBA public library, this is one of the largest hotels in the country. Rooms feature floor-to-ceiling windows, and are equipped with an iMac and free Wi-Fi, while the rooftop SkyLounge bar-restaurant offers a spectacular view across the city and harbour. Corporate clients are particularly well served, thanks to the business centre and convention facilities.

Grand Hotel Amrâth Amsterdam
Prins Hendrikkade 108-114, Waterfront (552 0000, www.amrathamsterdam. com). Tram 1, 2, 4, 5, 9, 13, 14, 16, 17, 26. **Map** *p154 N8.*
The Grand Hotel Amrâth nods handsomely to both Dutch sea-faring supremacy and the birth of an architectural movement. Considered the first example of the Amsterdam School, this century-old shipping office, known as the Scheepvaarthuis, bursts with creative brickwork and sculpture. The hotel's feeling of timelessness remains, although you can expect the usual range of deluxe frills, plus (a rarity here) a pool. Some rooms have supplements for specific views.

Hampshire Hotel Amsterdam American
Leidsekade 97, Grachtengordel (035 677 7217, www.hampshirehotel amsterdamamerican.com). Tram 1, 2, 5, 7, 10. **Map** *p97 G12.*
The public areas of this dazzling art nouveau monument are all eye-pleasers – especially the magnificently buttressed Café Américain. The rooms, though, are pretty cramped and decorated in smart-but-bland standard hotel fittings. They do have good views, either of the canal or the bustling square below, and some have their own balcony. Meeting facilities are available.

Mövenpick Hotel Amsterdam City Centre
Piet Heinkade 11, Waterfront (519 1200, www.movenpick.com). Tram 26. **Map** *p154 P7.*

Tall and glamorous, this striped, stone-coloured hotel is a great base for exploring Noord on the bank opposite. Rooms are decorated in soothing greys and woods; pricier ones grant access to an executive lounge and have great views over the city's rooftops, or of cruise liners ploughing through the waters.

Sir Albert Hotel
Albert Cuypstraat 2-6, De Pijp (305 3020, www.siralberthotel.com). Tram 16. **Map** *p165 J16.*
Once a diamond factory, Sir Albert is now a four-star 'luxury boutique' hotel featuring the interior stylings of BK Architects. High-ceilinged rooms are inspired by the great design movements of the past, while old-school service is balanced by the latest mod cons. Its Japanese pub-style restaurant, Izakaya, has been embraced by foodies.

Zoku Amsterdam
Weesperstraat 105, Plantage (811 2811, www.livezoku.com). Tram 7, 10 or Metro 51, 53, 54. **Map** *p143 N12.*
Described as a 'thriving neighbourhood for global nomads', the award-winning Zoku is designed as a hybrid live-and-work space to accommodate jet-setting entrepreneurs and mobile professionals. In addition to the funky co-working spaces, facilities include a music corner, games room, treatment room and a roof-terrace greenhouse. With commanding views of the city, the bar on the top floor is open to all.

Mid-range
Arena
's Gravesandestraat 55, Oosterpark (850 2400, www.hotelarena.nl). Tram 3, 7, 9, 10, 14. **Map** *p143 Q13.*
A holy trinity of hotel, restaurant and nightclub in a former Catholic orphanage, Arena is ideal for lazy young scenesters looking for a one-stop shop. The standard and large rooms are a bit boring from an aesthetic point of view; the extra-large ones and suites, kitted out by leading local designers, look great but come with a matching price

Suite Dreams

Fancy an alternative to a conventional hotel?

Amsterdam's hunger for new places to stay has resulted in some imaginative and unusual accommodation solutions.

'Boutique hostel' **Cocomama** (Westeinde 18, 627 2454, www. cocomamahostel.com) is located in a former brothel. In the past, it cost €200 for an hour of fun at the 'gentlemen's club' Princess; now it costs from €24 for a whole night. The rooms have been rebuilt to sleep groups of two to six; one room still suggests the house's rosy origins, while the others have been decorated with more traditional Dutch themes.

Crane Hotel Faralda (NDSM-Plein 78, 760 6161, www.faralda.nl) is a much posher and less down-to-earth (literally) affair. Three luxury double suites – 'Mystique', 'Free Spirit' and 'Secret' – have been built into the old crane that was once used to position ships in a dry dock at former shipyard NDSM. For €455 a night, you can enjoy all mod cons and amazing views of the city. You may also spot an international DJ or pop star, as it's a favourite for the famous faces who come to town.

In another industrial monument, over in the Westergasfabriek, the **Leidinghuis** (Klönneplein 1, 586 0711, www.westergasfabriek.nl) consists of two interconnected semi-circular buildings attached to the massive Gashouder, which once held gas and now holds events. Acclaimed Dutch designer – and king of recycled wood – Piet Hein

Eek designed the interior. There's a brilliant orange table downstairs, a kitchenette and library on the mezzanine, and a bathroom and bedroom nestled in the rafters. By day, it's used for workshops or parties, but it can also act as the ultimate suite for two. Rental costs from €200 for part of the day – double that to stay the night.

If it's more legendary Dutch design you're after, you can stay at **Hôtel Droog** (*see p84*). The Droog team originally planned to expand their shop to include a proper hotel, but were stymied by permit issues, so they ended up with just one suite. A lovely one, of course, that's filled with Droog design prototypes and much can be rented for around €200 per night. The suite is located in a pair of 17th-century buildings (formerly the city's STD clinic) that are divided into shop sections. The 'dining room' is a relaxing public café, a 'washroom' sells cosmetics and a 'wardrobe' features fashion.

If art is your thing, then stay in one of the growing number of design hotels. These include the Alice in Wonderland-themed **Andaz Amsterdam** (Prinsengracht 587, 523 1234, amsterdamprinsengracht. andaz.hyatt.com) – the love child of Dutch design maestro Marcel Wanders and hospitality super-group Hyatt – and **Art'otel Amsterdam** (Prins Hendrikkade 33, 719 7200 www.artotels.com), which is curated by Rotterdam artist Joep van Lieshout and has its own gallery.

tag. The location is a bit out of the way, but trams can whizz you into the centre in ten minutes.

CitizenM
Prinses Irenestraat 30, Zuid (811 7090, www.citizenm.com). Tram 5, 16. **Map** *off map.*

Welcome to the future of hotels: the shipping container. Due to the housing shortage in Amsterdam, local students have long been living in these humble units, but CitizenM is now using them as the basis for a 'budget luxury' designer-hotel chain. Created and assembled off-site, the 14sq m (150sq ft) rooms have a wall-to-wall window, a king-size bed with luxury linens, a shower pod, toilet pod and flatscreen TV. Refreshments are available 24/7 from the 'canteen'.

Hotel The Exchange
Damrak 50, Old Centre (523 0080, www.hoteltheexchange.com). Tram 1, 2, 4, 5, 9, 13, 16, 17. **Map** *p72 L8.*

A simple hallway leads back to a red gift-box of a reception, offering just a peek of the statement seating in the mezzanine above. Each of the 61 rooms in this hotel (graded from one to five stars) has been exquisitely dressed by designers from the Amsterdam Fashion Institute – and it shows.

Hotel Vondel
Vondelstraat 26-30, Museum Quarter (612 0120, www.hotelvondel.com). Tram 1, 2, 3, 5, 7, 10, 12, 16. **Map** *p129 F13.*

Another hidden gem near the museums and upmarket shopping opportunities, this thoroughly chic place is festooned with art and has a lovely decked garden. Rooms, ranging from small to huge, are designer-driven, with chandeliers and swanky bathrooms. Unusually for such a trendy hotel, families are encouraged.

Lloyd Hotel
Oostelijke Handelskade 34, Waterfront (561 3636, www.lloydhotel.com). Tram 10, 26. **Map** *p154 U8.*

This one-time youth prison has been reinvented as a stylish hotel offering one- to five-star accommodation, complete with a new 'cultural embassy'. Lloyd features the work of hotshot Dutch designers Atelier van Lieshout and Marcel Wanders. Expect the unexpected. The restaurant, with its sunny terrace and modishly simple menu, is a bonus. Its sibling is the fashion-conscious Hotel The Exchange (*see left*).

Volkshotel
Wibautstraat 150, Oost (261 2100, www.volkshotel.nl). Metro 51, 53, 54. **Map** *p143 P15.*

A 'hotel for the people', Volkshotel was a newspaper HQ in its former life, but now comprises 172 hotel rooms that range from cosy and simple to large and luxurious. Decor features glass, wood and concrete. A great place to stay if you're in town to party: the rooftop bar Canvas (*see p150*) offers views of the city and attracts boozing patrons until the wee hours.

Budget
Flying Pig Downtown
Nieuwendijk 100, Old Centre (420 6822, www.flyingpig.nl). Tram 1, 2, 4, 5, 9, 13, 16, 17, 26. **Map** *p72 L7.*

Young backpackers flock here from around the world, as much for the social life as the accommodation; the hostel organises free tours, and there are regular parties and cheap beer. Flying Pig hostels don't accept guests aged under 16 or over 40 – and our guess is that anyone over 30 will feel like a senior citizen. With locations near Leidseplein and at the beach in Noordwijk, you're sure to find multiple ways to party and make friends.

Hotel Casa
Eerste Ringdijkstraat 4, Oost (665 1171, www.hotelcasa.nl). Metro 51, 53, 54. **Map** *off map.*

Part-hotel, part-student housing, Hotel Casa attracts an eclectic mix of patrons. The concept was founded by four friends who wanted to create affordable living for students, but it grew to become the lively and inspiring hub it is today.

Hotel Prinsenhof
Prinsengracht 810, Grachtengordel (623 1772, www.hotelprinsenhof.com). Tram 4, 7, 10, 16. **Map** *p97 M13.*
A good option for budget travellers, this, ten-room hotel with helpful and friendly staff is right near the city's nightlife, and foodie Utrechtsestraat. The stairs are vertiginous – luggage is hauled up on a pulley. Rooms are simple, clean and tidy; some have shared facilities. Best of all, rooms with canal views don't attract a premium.

Stayokay Amsterdam Zeeburg
Timorplein 2, Oost (551 3190, www. stayokay.com). Tram 7, 14. **Map** *off map.*
Located in a grand old school building that also houses fab cinema and club Studio/K, this branch of the reliable hostel chain is done out in warm reds, with mosaic floors, sleek but simple furniture and huge photos on the walls. Perfect for families and the more discerning hosteller – HI members get a discount – check website for special packages.

Winston Hotel
Warmoestraat 129, Old Centre (623 1380, www.winston.nl). Tram 1, 2, 4, 5, 9, 14, 16. **Map** *p72 L8.*
The legendary Winston, now part of St Christopher's Inns, is renowned for its youthful, party-loving atmosphere and arty rooms decorated in an eclectic style by local artists. The dorms (of four, six

or eight beds) are much cheaper – but much less fun. There's also a late-opening bar on site and a club, Winston.

Other options
Longer-term accommodation options do exist, though the range isn't enormous and it can get pricey. Of course, **Airbnb** (www.airbnb.com) is always a good point of call. A few hotels have apartments, or you can try **Apartment Services** (www.apartment services.nl) or **StayAmsterdam** (www.stayamsterdam. com). **City Mundo** (amsterdam. citymundo.com) matches visitors to assorted accommodation – anything from a room in a flat to a houseboat or a traditional Dutch windmill.

Camping
Camping is a national pastime for the Dutch, so you can expect well-maintained sites with good facilities, including laundries and supermarkets. Situated north of the city centre is **Amsterdam City Camp** (Papaverweg 50, Noord, mob 06467 98022, www.amsterdamcitycamp. nl), a site exclusively for motorhomes next to the NDSM shipyard. **Zeeburg** (Zuider IJdijk 20, Zeeburg, 694 4430, www.campingzeeburg.nl) is a young people's site; **Gaasper** (Loosdrechtdreef 7, Zuidoost, 696 7326, www. gaaspercamping.nl) and **Amsterdamse Bos** (Kleine Noorddijk 1, Amstelveen (641 6868, www.campingamsterdam sebos.nl) are aimed at families, while everyone mixes happily together at **Vliegenbos** (Meeuwenlaan 138, Noord, 636 8855, www.vliegenbos.com).

Getting Around

ARRIVING & LEAVING

By air

Amsterdam's **Schiphol Airport** (794 0800, www.schiphol.nl) is 18km (11 miles) south-west of the city. There's only one terminal building, with four departure and arrival halls.

Taxis

A fixed fare from the airport to the south and west of the city costs around €40, and to the city centre about €50. There are always plenty of licensed taxis beside the main exit. You can book taxis on the Schiphol website.

Connexxion Airport Hotel Shuttle

Connexxion desk, Schiphol Plaza, near Arrivals Hall 4, Schiphol Airport (038 339 4741, www.schipholhotelsshuttle.nl). Departs from platform A7.
This bus from Schiphol to Amsterdam runs at least every 30 mins 6am-9.30pm. Anyone can buy a ticket (€17 single, €27 return), not just hotel guests. Drop-off points are the 100-odd allied hotels; see website for schedules.

Trains

Trains leave every 10 mins or so, 5am-midnight (after which they depart hourly). The journey to Centraal Station takes about 20 mins. Buy tickets (€4.20 single) before you board or you may incur a €35 fine. There's a €0.50 surcharge to buy tickets over the counter; use the machines (with English instructions) instead.

Airlines

Aer Lingus *0900 265 8207 premium rate, www.aerlingus.com*
Air Canada *0800 0229 769, www. aircanada.com*
Air France *654 5720, www.airfrance.com*

British Airways *346 9559, www. britishairways.com*
Delta Airlines *721 9128, www.delta.com*
EasyJet *0900 040 1048 premium rate, www.easyjet.com*
KLM *474 7747, www.klm.com*
Lufthansa *0900 123 4777 premium rate, www.lufthansa.com*
United Airlines *346 9381, www.united.com*

By car

Options for crossing the Channel with a car include: Harwich to Hook of Holland with **Stena Line** (www.stenaline.nl); Newcastle to Amsterdam (IJmuiden) with **DFDS Seaways** (www.dfdsseaways.co.uk); Hull to Rotterdam or Zeebrugge with **P&O Ferries** (www.poferries.com); and Dover to Calais with P&O Ferries. **Irish Ferries** from Ireland go from Rosslare to either Roscoff or Cherbourg in France (www.irishferries.com). Another option is the **Eurotunnel** to France (www.eurotunnel.com).

By coach

International coach services arrive at Amstel Station. To book a ticket, visit the **Eurolines** website (www.eurolines.com). Fares start from €25 for a single from London Victoria to Amsterdam.

By rail

The fastest route from London is to catch a **Eurostar** train (www.eurostar.com) from St Pancras International to Brussels, then change to an InterCity or Thalys high-speed train to Amsterdam. A much-delayed direct route between London and Amsterdam will bring the journey time down to just 4hrs.

The Dutch Flyer train and ferry service involves a train from Liverpool Street Station to Harwich, Stena Line's superferry crossing to Hook of

Holland, and then a train to Amsterdam Centraal (changing in Rotterdam).

If you live in the North of England or Scotland, take the ferry from Hull or Newcastle. Transfer buses shuttle from the port to either Rotterdam Centraal or Amsterdam Centraal stations.

PUBLIC TRANSPORT

Amsterdam is easy to get around. There are efficient, cheap and integrated trams, metros and buses, and in the centre most places can be reached on foot. Locals tend to get around by bike, and there are also boats and water taxis. Be warned that public transport provision for those with disabilities is dire. For information, tickets, maps and an English-language guide to public transport tickets, visit the website of **GVB**, Amsterdam's municipal transport authority (www.gvb.nl).

Trams are the best way to travel around the city by public transport, with a network of routes through the centre (buses and the metro are more useful for outlying suburbs). For a basic map of the tram network, *see inside back cover.*

Fares & tickets
An **OV-chipkaart** ('chip card', www. ov-chipkaart.nl) system operates across the tram, bus and metro network. The card, which is valid for five years, incurs a one-off €7.50 fee and can be purchased at station ticket machines, tobacconists and many supermarkets, as well as GVB Tickets & Info offices (www.gvb.nl). You load the card in the ticket vending machine, paying with cash or card, and use it immediately. You can also load the card in yellow Add Value Machines at various shops.

An unlimited 24-hour OV-chipkaart costs €7.50. You can also buy unlimited 48-, 72-, 96-, 120-, 144- and 168-hour cards (ranging from €12.50 to €34). With any type of OV-chipkaart, you have to check in and out when boarding or disembarking a tram, bus or metro, using the card readers in the trams and buses, at the entryway to metro stations

or on the metro platform. Hold your card in front of the reader and wait for a beep and green light to flash.

An alternative to the OV-chipkaart is the **Iamsterdam City Card**, which includes unlimited public transport and free entrance to 38 museums and attractions. It can be purchased at shops and newsagents across Amsterdam, or at one of the Iamsterdam tourist offices (*see p68*). The card costs €57 (24hrs), €67 (48hrs) or €77 (72hrs). Don't even think about travelling without a ticket: inspectors make regular checks, and passengers without tickets are hit with €37.50 on-the-spot fines.

Trams & buses
Trams run from 6am (6.30am Sat, 7.30am Sun). Night buses (nos.348-369) take over at other times. All night buses go to Centraal Station, except 369 (Station Sloterdijk to Schiphol Airport).

Night-bus stops are indicated by a black square with the bus number printed on it. During off-peak hours and at quiet stops, stick out your arm to let the driver know you want to get on. Signs at tram and bus stops show the name of the stop and line number, and boards indicate the full route.

Tram rules
Other road users need to be aware that a tram will only stop if absolutely necessary. Cyclists should listen for tram warning bells and cross tramlines at an angle to avoid the front wheel getting stuck. Motorists should avoid blocking tramlines: cars are allowed on them only if turning right.

Metro
The metro uses the same OV-chipkaart system as trams and buses (*see left*) and serves suburbs to the south and east. Three separate lines – 51, 53 and 54 – terminate at Centraal Station (sometimes abbreviated to CS), while line 50 connects west with south-east. Metro trains run from 6am (6.30am Sat, 7.30am Sun) to around 12.15am.

TAXIS

Your best bet is to opt for a cab with a red and black 'TCA/7x7' rooflight, or phone 777 7777.

Easiest places to hail a taxi are outside Centraal Station; alongside the bus station (at Kinkerstraat and Marnixstraat); Rembrandtplein; and Leidseplein. Always ask your driver how much your journey will cost before you set off. Make sure the meter starts at the minimum charge (€2.95); you're then charged €2.17/km. If you feel you've been cheated, ask for a receipt before handing over cash. If the fare seems too high, you can file a complaint (0900 202 1881 premium rate, 9am-5pm) or contact the police. Wheelchairs will only fit in taxis if they're folded. If you're a wheelchair user, you can call Van der Laan BV (647 4700, 24hrs daily).

Alternatively, hail a bicycle cab – basically a high-tech rickshaw – or one of the bright yellow water taxis that go up and down the canals.

DRIVING

If you're coming by car to the Netherlands, it's wise to join a national motoring organisation before you leave. To drive in the Netherlands, you'll need a valid national driving licence; ANWB and many car-hire firms favour photocard licences (Brits need the paper version as well for this to be legal). You'll need proof that your vehicle has passed a road safety test in its country of origin, an international identification disc, vehicle registration papers and insurance documents.

The Dutch drive on the right. Motorways are labelled 'A'; major roads 'N'; and European routes 'E'. Seatbelts are compulsory for drivers and all passengers. Speed limits are usually 50km/h (31mph) within cities, 80km/h (50mph) outside, and 100km/h (62mph) on motorways. Speeding and other traffic offences are subject to heavy on-the-spot fines.

If you're driving in Amsterdam, look out for cyclists. Many streets in Amsterdam are one-way – for cars, that is, not bikes, so don't be surprised to see people cycling against the traffic flow.

Strict drink driving laws only allow 0.5 mg of alcohol per ml of blood.

Car hire

Dutch car hire (*autoverhuur*) firms expect at least one year's driving experience and will want to see a valid national driving licence and passport before they hire a vehicle. All will require a deposit by credit card, and you generally need to be over 21. Prices given below are for one day's hire of the cheapest car available excluding insurance and VAT.

Diks Autoverhuur *Van Ostadestraat 278-280, De Pijp (662 3366, www.diks. net). Tram 3, 4.* **Open** *8am-7.30pm Mon-Sat; 9am-12.30pm, 8-10.30pm Sun.* **Map** *p165 L16.*
Cars from €28 per day. The first 150km are free, then it's €0.19/km.
Hertz *Overtoom 333, Oud West (612 2441, www.hertz.nl). Tram 1.* **Open** *8am-6pm Mon-Fri; 8am-2pm Sat; 9am-2pm Sun.* **Map** *p129 C14.*
Cars from €50 per day. The first 200km are free, then it's €0.18/km.

Parking

All of central Amsterdam is metered from 9am until at least 7pm – and in many places to midnight – and spaces are difficult to find, especially within the Grachtengordel. Official parking garages are often the easiest solution but are costly. For on-street parking, look for the blue boxes marked with a white 'P' to pre-pay with a credit card. You'll have to enter your registration – parking officials from Cition (the local traffic authority) then just scan the plate to see if you've paid. Depending on the area, you'll pay €3-€5/hr.

When leaving your car in the city, empty it of valuables and leave your glovebox open: cars with foreign plates are vulnerable to break-ins. Apps like Parkopedia can be useful to find cheaper parking places.

Car parks

Car parks are indicated by a white 'P' on a blue square sign. Also worth considering are the very economical Park and Rides (see www.bereikbaaramsterdam.nl for locations), which cost between €1 and €8 per day. For more information and a list of locations in English, see www.Iamsterdam.com/en/visiting/plan-your-trip/getting-around/parking.

P1 Parking Amsterdam Centraal *Prins Hendrikkade 20, Old Centre (638 5330, www.p1.nl).* **Open** *24hrs.* **Rates** *€5/hr; €55/24hrs.* **Map** *p72 L7.*

Q-Park Europarking *Marnixstraat 250, Jordaan (0900 446 6880 premium rate, www.q-park.nl).* **Open** *24hrs.* **Rates** *€2/23mins; €40/24hrs.* **Map** *p117 F10.*

Q-Park De Kolk *Nieuwezijds Kolk 18, Old Centre (0900 446 6880 premium rate, www.q-park.nl).* **Open** *24hrs.* **Rates** *€2/20mins; €52/24hrs.* **Map** *p72 K7.*

Parking fines

Fines are €38.10, plus the price of one hour's parking in that section of town, and can only be paid via your bank. For more details, visit www.amsterdam.nl/parkeren-verkeer/parkeerbon and click on 'parking'; include your registration and ticket number when transferring funds. If you suspect your car has been towed, call 14 020 (24hrs). If this is the case, you'll have to pay €373 plus €30/day. Payment only possible with a card.

Petrol

There are 24hr petrol stations (*tankstations*) at Gooiseweg 10, Sarphatistraat 225, Marnixstraat 250 and Spaarndammerdijk 218.

WATER TRANSPORT

Amsterdam is best seen from the water. For ways to get around, *see p98* **Canal**

Cruising. When renting a boat, stick to the right and beware of canal cruisers.

CYCLING

Cycling is the most convenient means of getting from A to B. There are plenty of good, cheap bike hire companies around, of which we list a selection below.

Bike rental

There are many places to rent a bike, for about €10 a day. A passport and/or credit card is required.

Bike City *Bloemgracht 68-70, Jordaan (626 3721, www.bikecity.nl).* Tram 10, 13, 14, 17. **Open** *9am-5.30pm daily.* **Rates** *from €13.50/day with €50 deposit.* **Map** *p117 G8.*

Frederic Rentabike *Brouwersgracht 78, Jordaan (www.frederic.nl, 624 5509).* Bus 18, 21, 22. **Open** *9am-5.30pm daily.* **Rates** *from €15/24hrs.* **Map** *p117 K6.*

King Bikes *Kerkstraat 143, Museum Quarter (422 1026, www.kingbikes. nl).* Tram 1, 2, 5, 7, 10, 16, 24. **Open** *9am-8pm daily.* **Rates** *from €10/24hrs.* **Map** *p129 J12.*

Mac Bike *Overtoom 45, Oud West (683 3369, www.macbike.nl).* Tram 1, 3, 12. **Open** *9am-6pm daily.* **Rates** *€9.75/24hrs.* **Map** *p129 F12.*

Mike's Bike Tours *Kerkstraat 134, Grachtengordel (622 7970, www. mikesbiketours amsterdam.com).* Tram 1, 2, 5. **Open** *Mar-Oct 9am-6pm daily. Nov-Feb 10am-6pm daily.* **Rates** *from €10/24hrs.* **Map** *p97 J12.*

Rent-A-Bike *Damstraat 20-22, Old Centre (625 5029, www.rentabike. nl).* Tram 4, 9, 14, 16. **Open** *9am-6pm daily.* **Rates** *€9.25/24hrs; €25 deposit and passport/ID card or credit card photocopy.* **Map** *p72 K9.*

StarBikes Rental *De Ruyterkade 143, Waterfront (www.starbikesrental.com, 620 3215).* Tram 1, 2, 4, 5, 13, 16, 17, 19, 26. **Open** *8am-7pm Mon-Fri; 9am-7pm Sat, Sun.* **Rates** *from €9/24hrs.* **Map** *p154 O7.*

Resources A-Z

ACCIDENT & EMERGENCY

Emergency numbers

In an emergency, call **112** (free from any phone) and specify police, fire service or ambulance. For helplines and hospitals, *see below*; for police stations, *see p185*.

In the event of an accident, go to the **eerste spoedhulp** (A&E) of any hospital (*ziekenhuis*). In the case of a minor accident, call 088 003 0600 (open 24/7) and the service will connect you with an emergency GP in your area. There's also the **Tourist Medical Service Amsterdam** (592 3355, touristdoctor.nl), which you can call 24hrs a day for free advice. You can also just turn up at the outpatient departments of the following city hospitals. All are open 24hrs a day, seven days a week.

Hospitals

Academisch Medisch Centrum
Meibergdreef 9, Zuid (566 9111, first aid 566 2222). Metro Holendrecht.
Boven IJ Ziekenhuis *Statenjachtstraat 1, Noord (634 6346, first aid 634 6200). Bus 34, 36, 37, 245.*
Onze Lieve Vrouwe Gasthuis (OLVG) *Oost Oosterpark 9, Oost (599 9111, first aid 599 3016). Tram 3, 7 or bus 37.*

OLVG West *Jan Tooropstraat 164, West (510 8911, first aid 510 8911). Tram 13 or bus 752.*
VU Ziekenhuis *De Boelelaan 1117, Zuid (444 4444, first aid 444 3636). Tram 16, 24 or bus 62, 246 or Metro Amstelveenseweg.*

AGE RESTRICTIONS

In the Netherlands, only those over the age of 18 can purchase alcohol, buy cigarettes, smoke cannabis or drive.

CUSTOMS

If you're entering the Netherlands from another EU country you may import goods for personal use. The following guidelines are for reference only:
• 800 cigarettes, 400 small cigars, 200 cigars or 1kg loose tobacco.
• 10l spirits (more than 22% alcohol), 20l of spirits (less than 22% alcohol), 90l of wine (or 60l of sparkling wine) or 110l of beer.

If you enter the country from a non-EU country, the following limits apply:
• 200 cigarettes or 250g of smoking tobacco or 100 cigarillos or 50 cigars (or a proportional assortment of these products).

Travel advice

For up-to-date information on travel to a specific country – including the latest on safety and security, health issues, local laws and customs – contact your home country government's department of foreign affairs. Most have websites with useful advice for would-be travellers.

Australia
www.smarttraveller.gov.au

Canada
www.voyage.gc.ca

New Zealand
www.safetravel.govt.nz

Republic of Ireland
foreignaffairs.gov.ie

UK
www.fco.gov.uk/travel

USA
www.state.gov/travel

- 1l of spirits or 2l of sparkling wine or 2l of fortified wine, such as sherry or port and 4l of non-sparkling wine and 16l of beer.
- Other goods to the value of €430.

The import of meat or meat products, fruit, plants, flowers and protected animals to the Netherlands is illegal. For more information, go to the English website of the tax authorities: www. belastingdienst.nl.

DISABLED

Winding cobbled streets, poorly maintained pavements and steep canal house steps can present real difficulties to the less physically able, but the pragmatic Dutch can generally solve problems quickly. Most large museums, cinemas and theatres have decent disabled facilities. The metro is accessible to wheelchair users with normal arm function, but most trams are inaccessible to wheelchair users due to their high steps. The website www. toegankelijk amsterdam.nl has a list of hotels, restaurants and attractions that cater well for the physically less able. **StarBikes** (*see p181*) also rents a special bicycle for the disabled.

DRUGS

Locals have a relaxed attitude to soft drugs, but smoking isn't acceptable everywhere. Use discretion. Outside Amsterdam, public consumption of cannabis is largely unacceptable. Foreigners found with hard drugs should expect to face prosecution. Organisations offering advice can do little to help foreigners with drug-related problems, although the **Jellinek Drugs Prevention Centre** can provide help in several languages, including English. Its helpline (590 1515, open 3-5pm Mon-Thur) offers advice and information. There's also a 24-hour crisis/detox number: 590 5000.

Climate

Average temperatures and monthly rainfall in Amsterdam.

	Temp (°C/°F)	Rainfall (mm/in)	Sun (hrs/day)
January	5.8/42.4	65/2.5	2
February	6.7/44	52/2	2
March	9.9/49.8	53/2.1	3
April	14.2/57.5	41/1.6	5
May	17.7/63.9	60/2.3	7
June	20.1/68.2	66/2.6	7
July	22.1/71.8	91/3.6	7
August	22.2/72	105/4.1	7
September	19/66.2	81/3.2	5
October	14.6/58.3	85/3.3	3
November	9.7/49.5	84/3.3	2
December	6/42.8	84/3.2	2

ELECTRICITY

Electricity in the Netherlands runs on 220V. Visitors with British 240V appliances can use an adaptor. For US 110V appliances, a transformer.

EMBASSIES & CONSULATES

American Consulate *General Museumplein 19, Museum Quarter (575 5309 8am-4.30pm daily, 070 310 2209 outside business hrs, netherlands/ usembassy.gov). Tram 3, 5, 12, 16, 24.* **Open** *US citizens' services 8.30-11.30am Mon-Fri. Immigrant visas by appt.*
Australian Embassy *Carnegielaan 4, The Hague (070 310 8200, Australian citizen emergency phone 0800 0224 794, netherlands.embassy.gov.au).* **Open** *8.30am-5pm Mon-Fri. Passport & notarial services 9am-1pm Mon-Fri.*
British Consulate *Koningslaan 44, Vondelpark, www.gov.uk/ government/world/netherlands). Tram 2.* **Open** *British citizens 9am-12.30pm Mon, Tue, Thur, Fri. Phone enquiries 9am-1pm, 2-4.30pm Mon-Fri. Visa enquiries by appt 3-4.30pm Mon-Fri.*
British Embassy *Lange Voorhout 10, The Hague (070 427 0427).* **Open** *9am-5.30pm Mon-Fri.*
Canadian Embassy *Sophialaan 7, The Hague (070 311 1600, www.netherlands. gc.ca).* **Open** *9am-1pm, 2-5.30pm Mon-Fri. Consular & passport section 9.30am-12.30pm Mon-Fri (afternoons by appt only).*
Irish Embassy *Scheveningseweg 112, The Hague (070 363 0993, www.embassyofireland.nl).* **Open** *10am-12.30pm, 2.30-5pm Mon-Fri. Visa enquiries 10am-12.30pm Mon-Fri.*
New Zealand Embassy *Eisenhowerlaan 77N, The Hague (070 346 9324, www.nzembassy.com/ netherlands).* **Open** *9am-12.30pm, 1.30-5.30pm Mon-Fri.*

See **embassy.goabroad.com** for all other embassies and consulates.

HEALTH

It's advisable that all travellers take out insurance before leaving home. EU residents travelling in Europe require a European National Health Insurance Card (EHIC). This allows them to benefit from free or reduced-cost medical care when in the European Economic Area (EEA) or Switzerland. The EHIC is free of charge. For further information, refer to www.dh.gov.uk/travellers and *p182* Accident & Emergency.

LANGUAGE

Dutch is the official language of the Netherlands, though most Dutch people speak English to a high standard.

LEFT LUGGAGE

There's a staffed left-luggage counter at **Schiphol Airport** (795 2843, www. schiphol.nl), where you can store luggage for up to one month, open 24hrs daily (€7/24hrs). There are also automatic left-luggage lockers, accessible 24hrs a day (from €6/24hrs, for up to 168hrs). There are also plenty of lockers at **Centraal Station**, with 24hr access (from €7/24hrs).

LGBT

Gay & Lesbian Switchboard *623 6565, www.switchboard.nl)* Advice on everything in perfect English.
Pink Point Westermarkt *Grachtengordel (428 1070).* **Open** *10.30am-6pm daily.* All queer queries covered.

LOST PROPERTY

Report lost property, especially a lost passport or ID card, to the police. Inform your embassy or consulate, too, if you lose your passport.
Centraal Station *Stationsplein 15, Old Centre (030 751 5155, www.ns.nl). Tram 1, 2, 4, 5, 9, 13, 16, 17, 24, 26.* **Open** *24hrs daily.*
Items found on trains are kept for five days at the station (0900 321 2100

premium rate), after which they're forwarded to the Centraal Bureau Gevonden Voorwerpen (Central Lost Property Office) in Utrecht (www. nshispeed.nl, 8am-5pm Mon-Fri), where they're stored for three months.

GVB Lost Property *Arlandaweg 100 (0900 8011 premium rate, 9am-7pm Mon-Sat; en.gvb.nl/klantenservice/ verloren-voorwerpen). Tram 12 or Bus 15, 22, 36, 61, 69, 231, 269, 748 or Sloterdijk rail. Open 9am-5pm Mon-Wed; 9am-7pm Thur.*

Wait a day or two before you call and describe what you've lost on the bus, metro or tram. If your property has been found, you can pick it up at GVB head office at Arlandaweg.

Municipality Lost Property *Korte Leidsedwarsstraat 52 (251 0222). Tram 1, 2, 5, 7, 10. Open In person 9am-4pm Mon-Fri. By phone noon-4pm Mon-Fri.*

MONEY

Since January 2002 the Dutch currency has been the euro.

ATMs

Cash machines are found at banks, supermarkets and larger shops such as HEMA. You should be able to withdraw cash from ATMs using any credit or debit card.

Banks

Most banks are open 9am-5pm, Mon-Fri, with Postbank opening on Sat morning as well. Dutch banks buy and sell foreign currency, but few give cash advances against credit cards.

Credit cards

Most restaurants take cards; they're less popular in bars and shops, and some supermarkets don't accept them at all, so always carry some cash. If you lose your card, call the relevant 24hr number:

American Express *504 8000*
MasterCard *0800 022 5821*
Visa *0800 022 3110*

Tax

Sales tax (BTW) – 21 per cent on most items, six per cent on goods such as books and food – will be included in prices quoted in shops.

OPENING HOURS

As a general rule, shops open 1pm-6pm Mon (if at all); 9/10am-6pm Tue-Fri, with some open until 9pm Thur; and 9am-5pm Sat. Many are open on Sun. The city's bars open at various times and close at around 1am throughout the week, except for Fri and Sat, when they stay open until 2am or 3am. Restaurants generally open 5-11pm; many are closed on Sun and Mon.

PHARMACIES

Chemists (*drogists*) are usually open 9.30am-5.30pm Mon-Sat. For prescription drugs, go to a pharmacy (*apotheek*).

Apotheek Leidsestraat *Leidsestraat 74-76, Grachtengordel (422 0210, www. leidsestraat apotheek .nl). Tram 1, 2, 5. Open 8.30am-11pm daily.*

Sint Lucas Andreas Apotheek *Jan Tooropstraat 164, West (510 8826, www.sintlucasandreas ziekenhuis.nl/ afdeling/apotheek). Tram 13, bus 752. Open 24hrs daily.*

POLICE

For emergencies, call 112. There's also a 24-hr police service line (0900 8844) for the Amsterdam area. Dutch police (www.politie.nl) can hold people for up to 6hrs for questioning for minor crimes, 24hrs for major matters – but they'll phone the relevant consulate on behalf of a foreign detainee.

Hoofdbureau van Politie (Police Headquarters) *Lijnbaansgracht 219, Grachtengordel (0900 8844 premium rate). Tram 1, 2, 5, 7, 10. Open 24hrs daily. Map p97 G12.*

POSTAL SERVICES

All but one of the post offices in Amsterdam have closed. Instead, many book shops, tobacconists and supermarkets offer postal services. Look for the orange illuminated sign with the PostNL logo. The remaining office is at *Singel 250, Grachtengordel (www. postnl.nl)*. **Open** *8am-6.30pm Mon-Fri; 9am-5pm Sat*. **Map** *p109, J9*

PUBLIC HOLIDAYS

Known as *Nationale Feestdagen* in Dutch.
Nieuwjaarsdag *New Year's Day* 1 Jan
Goede Vrijdag *Good Friday*
Eerste Paasdag *Easter Sunday*
Tweede Paasdag *Easter Monday*
King's Day 27 Apr
Bevrijdingsdag *Liberation Day* 5 May
Hemelvaartsdag *Ascension Day*
Pinksteren *Whit Sunday/Pentecost*
Pinkstermaandag *Whit Monday*
Eerste Kerstdag *Christmas* 25 Dec
Tweede Kerstdag *Boxing Day* 26 Dec

SMOKING

In 2008, the Netherlands imposed a smoking ban in all public indoor spaces. As for cannabis, smoking it isn't acceptable everywhere in the city. If in doubt, ask before you spark up.

TELEPHONES

We list Amsterdam numbers without the city code, which is 020. To call within the city, just dial the seven-digit number. To phone Amsterdam from elsewhere in the Netherlands add 020 at the start of the number. Numbers in the Netherlands outside Amsterdam are listed with their code. There are other types of numbers that appear in this book. 06 numbers are for mobile phones; 0800 numbers are freephone numbers; and 0900 numbers are premium rate.

Dialling & codes
From the Netherlands
Dial the following code, then the number.
Australia *00 61*
Irish Republic *00 353*
UK *00 44 (then drop the first '0' from the area code)*
USA & Canada *00 1*

To the Netherlands
Use the country code 31, followed by the number. Drop the first '0' of the area code. The first 0 on mobiles is also dropped.
From Australia *00 11 31*
From UK & Irish Republic *00 31*
From USA *011 31*

Mobile phones
Check with your service provider before leaving your home country about service while you're in the Netherlands.

TIME

The Netherlands is an hour ahead of Greenwich Mean Time (GMT). The Dutch use the 24-hour clock.

TIPPING

It's polite to round up to the nearest euro for small bills or the nearest five for larger sums, although tipping 10% is becoming more common.

TOURIST INFORMATION

Iamsterdam Visitor Information
Stationsplein 10, Old Centre (702 6000, www.Iamsterdam.com). Tram 1, 2, 4, 5, 9, 13, 16, 17, 24, 26. **Open** *9am-5pm Mon-Sat; 10am-4pm Sun*.
Other location Schiphol Airport, Arrivals Hall 2 (7am-10pm daily).

VISAS & IMMIGRATION

Citizens from the EU, USA, Canada, Australia and New Zealand need a valid passport for stays of less than three months. Citizens of other countries must have a tourist visa. For stays longer than three months, apply for a resident's permit at the **Immigration and Naturalisation Service** (Stadhouderskade 85, 088 043 0430, www.ind.nl).

WEIGHTS & MEASURES

The Dutch use metric weights, distances and measurements.

Index

Picture credits

Credits

Crimson credits

Authors Lizzie Mulherin, Steve Korver
Editor Camilla Cary-Elwes
Proofreader Jo Williams
Picture Researcher Kate Michell
Layouts Emilie Crabb, Patrick Dawson
Cartography Gail Armstrong, Simonetta Giori

Series Editor Sophie Blacksell Jones
Production Manager Kate Michell
Design Mytton Williams

Chairman David Lester
Managing Director Andy Riddle

Advertising Media Sales House
Marketing Lyndsey Mayhew-Dehaney
Sales Molly Keel

Acknowledgements

The authors and editors would like to thank Nachtburgemeester Mirik Milan, plus all contributors to previous editions of *Time Out Amsterdam* whose work forms the basis of this guide.

Photography credits

Front cover Getty Images/iStockphoto
Back cover photo.ua/Shutterstock.com
Interior Photography credits, *see p191*.

Publishing information

Time Out Amsterdam Shortlist 5th edition
© TIME OUT ENGLAND LIMITED 2017
July 2017

ISBN 978-1-78059-250-3
CIP DATA: A catalogue record for this book is available from the British Library

Published by Crimson Publishing
19-21c Charles Street, Bath,
BA1 1HX (01225 584 950,
www.crimsonpublishing.co.uk) on behalf of Time Out England.

Distributed by Grantham Book Services
Distributed in the US and Canada by Publishers Group West (1-510-809-3700)

Printed by Grafostil